Praise for *The End of the Everything Bubble*

"Take a tour through Sandy Nairn's well-curated, well-annotated financial picture gallery. The images should frighten you. Better still if they also catalyze prudent, wealth-saving action. A timely warning by an investor who knows whereof he speaks."

– James Grant, editor of *Grant's Interest Rate Observer*

"The scale of monetary and fiscal expansion in recent years has been staggering, and has been much more successful in creating a boom in asset prices than growth in the real economy. Sandy Nairn's rigorous analysis of asset markets is compelling, and his conclusion that asset prices are set for a hard landing is persuasive."

– Lord Macpherson, former Permanent Secretary to H M Treasury

"In this book, Sandy Nairn eloquently describes the contours of the vast moral hazard landscape in which we are enveloped. This highly readable account of our predicament begs the question, is this the moment for a fundamental breakdown of the post-Bretton Woods economic and financial settlement? He has thrown down the gauntlet to the governing authorities, the major central banks and to his fellow-professionals in the investment industry, challenging them to provide a credible alternative, and more reassuring, appraisal of the status quo."

– Peter Warburton, director of Economic Perspectives Ltd and author of *Debt and Delusion*

The End of the Everything Bubble

Every owner of a physical copy of this edition of

The End of the Everything Bubble

can download the eBook for free direct from us at Harriman House, in a DRM-free format that can be read on any eReader, tablet or smartphone.

Simply head to:

ebooks.harriman-house.com/endoftheeverythingbubble

to get your copy now.

The End of the Everything Bubble

Why $75 trillion of investor wealth is in mortal jeopardy

Sandy Nairn

CEO OF EDINBURGH PARTNERS

HARRIMAN HOUSE LTD
3 Viceroy Court
Bedford Road
Petersfield
Hampshire
GU32 3LJ
GREAT BRITAIN
Tel: +44 (0)1730 233870

Email: enquiries@harriman-house.com
Website: harriman.house

First published in 2021.

Paperback ISBN: 978-0-85719-964-5
eBook ISBN: 978-0-85719-965-2

British Library Cataloguing in Publication Data
A CIP catalogue record for this book can be obtained from the British Library.

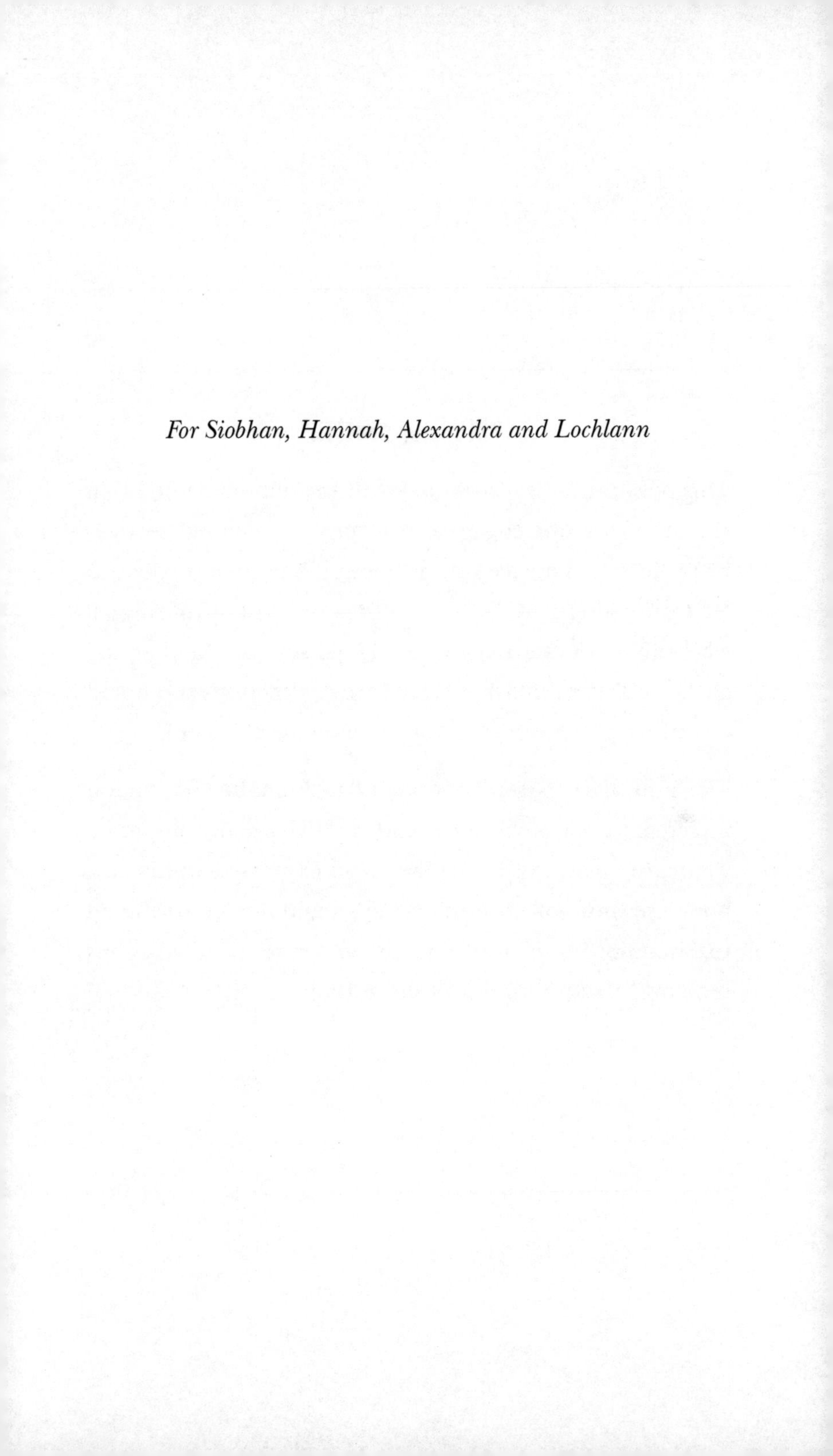

For Siobhan, Hannah, Alexandra and Lochlann

DISCLAIMER

“ ‘Since we decided a few weeks ago to adopt the leaf as legal tender, we have, of course, all become immensely rich…But we have also,’ continued the management consultant, ‘run into a small inflation problem on account of the high level of leaf availability…So in order to obviate this problem,’ he continued, ‘and effectively revalue the leaf, we are about to embark on a massive defoliation campaign, and…er, burn down all the forests. I think you’ll all agree that’s a sensible move under the circumstances.’ The crowd seemed a little uncertain about this for a second or two until someone pointed out how much this would increase the value of the leaves in their pockets whereupon they let out whoops of delight and gave the management consultant a standing ovation.”

– Douglas Adams, *The Restaurant at the End of the Universe*
(Pan Books, 1980)

Contents

About the Author

ALASDAIR (SANDY) NAIRN is one of the founders of Edinburgh Partners, an independent fund management company which was acquired by Franklin Templeton in 2018. Prior to establishing Edinburgh Partners he was chief investment officer of Scottish Widows Investment Partnership, and between 1990 and 2000 was employed by Templeton Investment Management where he was executive vice president and director of global equity research.

Before joining Templeton Investment Management, Sandy spent four years at Murray Johnstone as a portfolio manager and research analyst. Prior to that, he spent a year as an economist at the Scottish Development Agency. He is currently Investment Partner and CEO of Edinburgh Partners and Chairman of the Templeton Global Equity Group.

Sandy graduated from the University of Strathclyde and has a PhD in economics from the University of Strathclyde/ Scottish Business School. He is a CFA charterholder with the CFA Institute, and in 2020 he was elected a Fellow of the Royal Society of Edinburgh.

In 2001, he published the first edition of the investment classic *Engines That Move Markets*, a historical study of how technological advances can lead to stock market booms and busts, with the updated second edition being published in 2018. He has won multiple performance awards for the management of global equity portfolios over his 37-year investment career. In 2012 he co-authored the book *Templeton's Way With Money* with Jonathan Davis.

For the avoidance of doubt, all opinions expressed in this book are the sole responsibility of the author, as are any errors or omissions.

Preface

ALTHOUGH INFREQUENT, PERIODS of financial excess are hardly unknown in modern experience. My generation has lived through two of the worst peacetime economic crises of modern times – the global inflation shock of the 1970s and the global banking crisis of 2008 – as well as two other notable but less severe recessions in 1989–90 and 1999–2000.

In all four episodes the stock market suffered a sharp decline and economic activity took a big hit. While there will always be cycles in the economy and in financial markets, their impact on people's livelihoods and wealth can be compounded if there is financial exuberance in the years preceding declines.

It appears obvious to me that another such period of exuberance is unfolding before our eyes.

When policymakers began responding to the global pandemic in 2020, the hope was that we could avoid a repeat of damaging and avoidable market crashes witnessed in 2000 and 2008, where rampant speculation and irresponsible lending contributed to 50% declines in stock market wealth. These episodes rightly bear comparison with the great financial crises of the more distant past – 1873, 1896, 1907 and 1929 among them.

It would be comforting to think the lessons of the past have been learned. It has been clear for some time, however, that they have not. Global leaders, both politicians and central bankers, have locked themselves into a policy box from which even an economic Houdini would struggle to escape. The effect has been to induce yet again the kind of widespread financial excess that has precipitated damaging declines in the past.

It means we are heading for another painful period in which financial losses will spread through the markets, not only causing losses for investors, but spilling over into the real economy. As an investor who believes history has much to teach us, I find the current complacency of politicians, bankers and many professional investors about this prospect deeply concerning.

Signs of excess are visible all around. You can see it in the price of Bitcoin, in the exalted levels of share prices, in the mania for online gambling, in any number of crazy 'blind pool' investments that nobody could sensibly want to own

– and, in fact, in the majority of investment assets, from classic cars to modern art.

These are clear echoes of the dangerous behaviour which preceded the great stock market crashes of the past. Many of these featured in my book, *Engines That Move Markets*,[1] a study of periods of technological boom and bust and their impact on financial markets, ranging from the early 19th century to the present day.

Much of the data used in the following pages refers to the US. This is not intended to suggest that the rest of the world is not equally important. Nor does it mean that when the cracks appear they will necessarily appear first in North America. The focus on the US is mainly to help present a consistent picture for the world's largest and most dynamic economy. It is partly also because it is where many of the signs of asset price excess are most evident.

The purpose of writing this analysis is to draw attention to the risks facing investors in today's world and to lay out some of the options open to those who are willing to act now to avoid future harm to their wealth. The right course of action will depend on which of a number of scenarios play out.

Of course, my assumptions and line of reasoning may be wrong. It could be that the world can muddle through for a little while longer. Yet history tells us that wishful thinking,

---

1 Nairn, A., 2018. *Engines That Move Markets: Technology Investing from Railroads to the Internet and Beyond.* 2nd ed. Petersfield: Harriman House.

while good for morale, is rarely a productive approach in investment. The prudent will be taking remedial action today.

ALASDAIR NAIRN
Edinburgh, 2021

1.
Exceptional Times

WE ARE LIVING through an extraordinary period that in many respects has no parallel in the history of financial markets. These are some of the striking features of current market conditions as we enter the new decade, 13 years on from the global financial crisis of 2008:

- Interest rates are the lowest they have been for centuries and perhaps, according to one respected authority,[2] the lowest they have been for 5,000 years.[3]
- Governments have borrowed more money and accumulated more debt than at any previous time in history – with the US, for example, scaling the heights of its World War II peak.
- Central banks have created money and added monetary stimulus since the end of the global financial crisis on a scale that is greater than anyone has seen – or even thought possible – before.

---

2 Haldane, A., 2015. *Stuck*, Milton Keynes, Open University.

3 Sylla, R. and Homer, S., 2013. *A History of Interest Rates*. Hoboken, N.J.: Wiley.

- Governments are now embarking on an unprecedented peacetime fiscal expansion in response to slowing economic growth and the shock of the Covid-19 coronavirus pandemic.

- Although it has never been tried before, and despite its evident risks, the scale of this combined monetary and fiscal stimulus nevertheless appears to be supported by consensus elite opinion.

- Owners of debt have shown themselves willing to lend money on riskier terms and to riskier ventures than has been considered prudent in the past.

- $18 trillion, or over one quarter, of global investment-grade corporate bonds traded on negative nominal yields in October 2020, while the amount of sovereign debt selling on negative real yields exceeded $31trn. The real yield on US Treasuries has been negative for most of the past two years.

- Stock market valuations are at extreme levels, between two and three standard deviations above the historical mean, and not far removed from the excesses that preceded the 1929 and 2000 stock market crashes.

- Numerous other examples of speculation and financial excess can be observed across many types of investment assets and in the behaviour of financial institutions and individuals alike. Bitcoin is a representative example, but there are many others.

It is only a question of when, not if, this period of high valuations and widespread speculation comes to a juddering halt. Looking back at past episodes when similar conditions applied, it seems extremely unlikely that the process of rectifying today's excesses can be anything but a painful one.

Not a new phenomenon

We have been here before. Periods of financial excess are easy to recognise, at least in retrospect. Typically they are named after their most salient characteristic. The 'Nifty Fifty' in the 1960s, Japanese real estate in the 1980s, the Asian crisis in the 1990s and the TMT (telecoms, media and technology) bubble in 2000 are some obvious examples. Sub-prime mortgage lending in the run-up to the global financial crisis of 2008 would be another.

A common feature of past crises is that governments – or, more recently, not-so-independent central banks – have been slow to react to the evidence of excessive risk-taking and asset-price inflation. In the famous words of a former chairman of the Federal Reserve, they fail to "take away the punch bowl" before the party gets out of hand. As a result, the hangover when it comes is longer and more painful than it might have been.

Periods of overvaluation are typically followed by a period of cleansing during which assets return to more normal levels. The most damaging episodes of all are those which cause wider collateral damage by intensifying recessions and bringing down the price of other assets as well, not just those which precipitated the crisis.

The magnitude of the damage depends very much on the extent to which leverage has driven prices up. Debt is the booster rocket fuel that creates stock market bubbles and precipitates the worst market and economic declines. The rapid explosion in debt over the past decade is what makes the current situation so full of menace.

Although they may have ended in disaster, it would be a mistake to view past periods of financial excess solely as examples of collective lunacy. The journey from boom to bust often begins with legitimate logic. What then happens is that, as more and more investors buy into the argument, the logical trend slowly but surely intensifies until it reaches a point where the primary driver of rising prices ceases to be the original logic and the trend instead develops a momentum all of its own. The availability of cheap debt, itself sometimes the consequence of government policies conceived with quite a different objective in mind, compounds the problem.

A good example is the Japanese stock market and real estate bubble of the late 1980s. While the background was the growth of a successful and dynamic economy, the origins of the bubble lay in an international currency agreement, the Plaza Accord of 1985, which was designed to halt the rapid appreciation of the dollar in the early 1980s in the aftermath of the Federal Reserve's high interest rate attack on inflation.

The policy was eminently successful in the sense that it led to a steady fall in the value of the dollar and a consequent strengthening of the yen, Japan's currency. The logical response of the Japanese authorities was to try and help the country's exporters by offsetting the currency appreciation with easy credit and low interest rates.

All that did, however, was send the valuations of real estate companies, banks and companies with real estate assets (such as railroads and companies with land in the Tokyo Bay area) soaring. At one stage it was estimated that the Imperial Palace in Tokyo was worth more than the entire state of California. Real estate in Tokyo was trading at a price per square foot 350× that of Manhattan. In 1988 the Australian embassy in Tokyo sold its tennis courts for A$640 million.[4]

Although the overvaluation of Japanese assets was widely commented on at the time, it did not stop investors continuing to chase what seemed to be inexorable rises in the price of property and shares, often with money borrowed at dirt-cheap rates. One might think that professional investors, well aware of the stratospheric valuations, would have resisted the temptation to invest their clients' funds.

---

4 Fraser, A. and Coelle, A., 1988. Embassy sale nets $640m. *Canberra Times.*

Sadly not.

Professional investors are judged on performance relative to a benchmark index. Japan was the largest component of this index and rising sharply. The career risk of lagging the benchmark index, the so called 'curse of the index' was significant. When career risk and investment risk face off, for most it is an unequal battle. Career risk prevails. This was true then and it remains so today.

It was not until 1992 that the debt-fuelled asset bubble finally burst, condemning the Japanese economy, saddled as it now was with mountains of debt and near-bankrupt banks, to two decades of slow economic growth. The Japanese stock market has yet to regain its highs of 30 years ago.

Although the causes are different, the parallels with today are obvious, with one added twist. Normally in such crises the excess is largely confined to a particular geography or sectors and there is only limited impact on other parts of the economy, rather than generalised across the whole set of asset classes.

Consequently, even when we have 'bubbles', there may still be opportunities for investors who are willing to go hunting for value in the unloved areas of the market that have been neglected because of investor focus on the fashionable sector of the day.

What is distinctive, indeed unique, this time round is that we are witnessing an explosive growth of debt and excessive speculation across almost the entire universe of investable assets, not just in some particular sectors. The traditional defensive asset to which investors flee during crises is government bonds, but the bond market is at the epicentre of the looming crisis. With government borrowing at record peacetime levels and bond yields not far above zero, that traditional safety net is no longer there. For this reason the 'everything bubble' is an apposite description.

The heart of the problem

The root causes of periods of financial market excess are clearly many and varied, but in most instances low interest rates are one of the key factors underpinning asset-price inflation. Low interest rates are a common denominator in market bubbles and all too often cheap money, as we have seen, is the result of deliberate, but misguided and short-sighted, policymaking.

Is it the same this time? The answer is clearly *yes.* At the heart of the problem today is not just the fact that money has never been so cheap, but that policymakers, in both governments and central banks, have left themselves with little or no room to manoeuvre out of the trap they have set themselves by deliberately keeping the cost of money so low for so long.

The explanation for this state of affairs is not hard to find. It flows from the impact of the global financial crisis (GFC) in 2008. The GFC, with its uncomfortable similarities to the years leading up to the Great Depression, elicited a policy response which set out, at all costs, to avoid a repeat of the 1930s.

In that narrow sense, policy has been a success. Since the GFC almost any sign of weakness in the world economy has been met with a strong reaction from monetary authorities across the globe. Through a mixture of interest-rate cuts and quantitative easing (QE), monetary stimulus has been applied on an unprecedented scale.

So, while many feared that the financial crisis would produce a slump, the world economy has continued to grow, albeit slowly. A rerun of the deflationary experience of the 1930s has been averted. Critics of the policy response argued that monetary policy was too loose and would inevitably lead to higher consumer-price inflation.

This was faulty analysis. In the event, the GFC response has so far had little impact on consumer prices. Inflation has been conspicuous by its absence and remains at or below the central banks' target rate of 2% per annum.

The troubling aspect of this, however, is that what began as a temporary policy response to avert a potential collapse of the global banking system has mutated over time into something very different. Over the course of the last decade, monetary stimulus – whether in the form of interest rate cuts or QE – has become an automatic response to any negative market signal, and the knowledge that this is the case has, over time, become dangerously embedded in financial-market thinking.

The lack of inflation has encouraged central bankers to persevere with their easy policy stance, primarily because doing so appears to have no costs attached. We have moved into a world in which it is seen to be riskless for governments and businesses to increase the amount of debt they take on.

They are right in one sense: given how cheap money remains, the cost of servicing new and existing debt keeps falling. The ratio of government debt interest payments to GDP has paradoxically rarely been lower.

This is only so because we have what appear to be the lowest interest rates in 5,000 years of history. True, there may appear to be a degree of hyperbole in this statement, which originated from comments made by Andy Haldane, the then Chief Economist at the Bank of England:

"At a Parliamentary Committee hearing a few years ago I asserted, boldly, that global interest rates were at their lowest-ever levels. A wise colleague challenged me afterwards: 'How do you know they weren't lower in Babylonian times?' Several exhausted research assistants later, I can report that, luckily, I was on safe ground. Interest rates appear to be lower than at any time in the past 5000 years."[5]

---

5 Haldane, A., 2015. *Stuck*.

However, we do not need to refer as far back as Babylonian times for evidence. The Bank of England has also produced an 800-year record (figure 1). That interest rates are at, or around, historic lows is not in doubt.

But nor, crucially, is it an accident. The fear of a repeat of the Great Depression has resulted in a deliberate policy by the authorities to keep interest rates suppressed, a policy that has endured for more than 13 years, long after its initial rationale passed. For example, in 2015 Haldane argued that 'dread risk' – the emotional scarring of an event like the global financial crisis – may have contributed to the initial widespread sense of insecurity that required the anchoring of interest rates. Such events, he argued, "can exaggerate and prolong risk perceptions".[6]

We are now six years further on from the time of his speech and conditions are different. Prior to the global coronavirus pandemic in early 2020, the risk of a repeat of the 1930s had manifestly receded even further – yet the policy remained unchanged. The pandemic may have introduced a new dread risk into the equation. We cannot know for certain whether central bankers would have started to cut back their monetary stimulus earlier had the virus not struck.

As it is, their immediate response to the pandemic was to cut interest rates again and relaunch QE on a massive scale. As before, the response successfully staved off another global depression. More than a year later, thanks to the

6 Haldane, A., 2015. *Stuck.*

development of several effective vaccines, it is clear that the global economy is well on the way to recovery and asset prices have rebounded strongly, with many stock markets hitting new all-time highs.

Figure 1: Short- and long-term interest rates

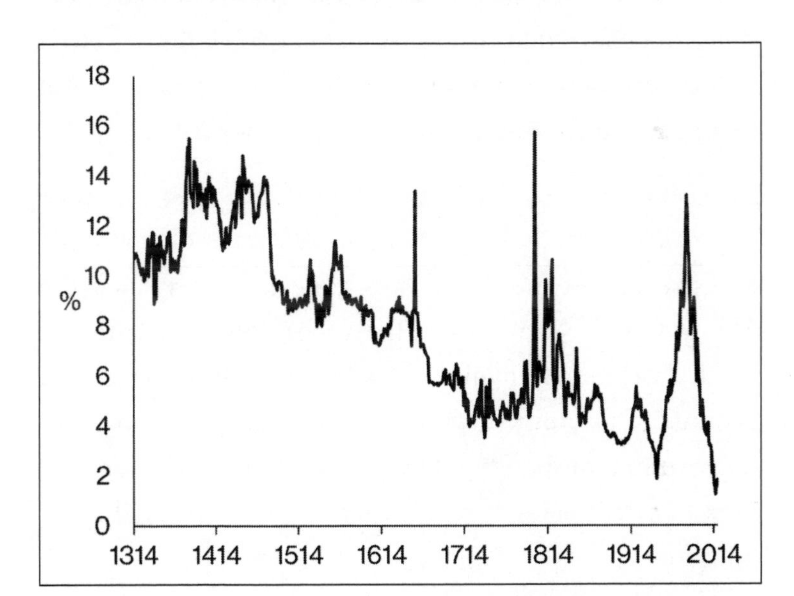

Source: GFD, Paul Schmelzing, 'Eight Centuries of Global Real interest Rates, R-G, and the "suprasecular" decline, 1311–2018,' Bank of England Staff Working Paper No. 845

Yet the suppression of interest rates continues. Thanks to the decline in bond yields, governments have so far been able repeatedly to refinance their expensive historic debt obligations at much lower rates of interest. As noted above, there appears to have been no penalty for taking on more debt, however imprudent it might have been thought by earlier generations.

Bolstered by this, governments have gradually abandoned the austerity policies that they adopted to pay for the intervention in the immediate aftermath of the global financial crisis. At that time it was thought that it made little sense to believe that the global debt crisis could be solved by the addition of yet more debt. Yet that paradoxical outcome, it turns out, has become the new orthodoxy.

Far from cutting back their need for debt finance, governments have committed to a range of spending and investment measures on a scale not seen since the very different conditions of the 1930s. With the outbreak of the Covid pandemic in early 2020, and the severe economic slowdown it precipitated, the impulse to ramp up government spending has only intensified. The amount of public debt being issued has leapt commensurately.

Wider systemic factors

In the background meanwhile have been some important changes in the global economic environment that are creating new risks. A number of trends that have acted as deflationary forces since the 1990s appear to be on the point of reversing, raising the danger that the benign inflationary conditions which have persisted for the past 30 years will soon be a thing of the past.

These trends have been positive for productivity improvements and economic growth until now, but they will increasingly start to act as headwinds to further economic advance.

Here are some of those headwinds:

- The world's population is ageing. In most major economies the dependency ratio – the number of those not of working age divided by the total working-age population – is worsening, meaning there are proportionately fewer workers to carry the burden of the economically inactive.
- The planet is warming. The threat of global warming requires a move away from fossil fuels and hydrocarbon-based activities. Whilst necessary, this will come at a financial cost in the medium term, even if the replacement technologies eventually drop in price.
- Migration flows are being inhibited by rising populism and political factors, as a result of which labour markets are no longer as freely and globally competitive as before.
- The flood of labour crossing borders after the fall of the Soviet Union, the expansion of the EU and the integration of China into the global economic system is now much more subdued.

- The productivity gains from rural-to-urban population movement and industrialisation in China (and Asia generally) will be much more limited in the future.
- The willingness of companies to rely on components and raw materials supplied by a single source is reversing, based on the realisation that having an extended supply chain without alternative suppliers carries serious strategic risks.

These powerful trends are also producing big changes in political behaviour. Faith in the free market is being replaced across the globe by support for ever greater government intervention – a trend that the pandemic has intensified. Recent experience has lent credibility to the idea that governments and central banks can fix most problems. This has not historically proved to be an effective approach to creating economic growth and profitability.

2.
Richly Valued Markets

Markets don't know or don't care

WHAT THIS ALL means is that the framework for pricing investment assets today is very different from the norm in previous financial history. Given the backdrop of high valuations and soaring debt, investors in both stock and bond markets should by rights be concerned. Yet that is not the picture you will gain from studying the performance of the two markets, which appear increasingly to be losing touch with reality.

Just as with Japan in the 1980s, the easy-money response to the global financial crisis has engendered huge momentum behind asset-price inflation. This is not necessarily illogical. At a theoretical level some form of 'risk-free' asset is needed to value financial assets. Typically government debt is used as the lowest default risk. In a world where the yield on this instrument has been suppressed for well over a decade, it should perhaps not be surprising that it has served to inflate all asset prices.

The combination of fiscal and monetary stimulus on a grand scale, accompanied by record-low interest rates, has created a combustible state of affairs. Noting the apparent willingness of policymakers to step in at the first sign of any market weakness to minimise losses, investors are throwing caution to the wind. It is hard to envisage a set of circumstances more likely to produce excessive risk-taking and unsustainable valuations in financial assets.

Stock markets

Valuations of leading stock markets are extremely elevated on virtually all conventional measures. Whether you are measuring price-to-book value, price-to-free cash flow, price-to-earnings, or Tobin's Q (which compares share prices to the replacement cost of assets) – all show high levels of valuation, well above historical norms.

Figure 2: Valuations above historical norms

(a) US price-to-book ratio

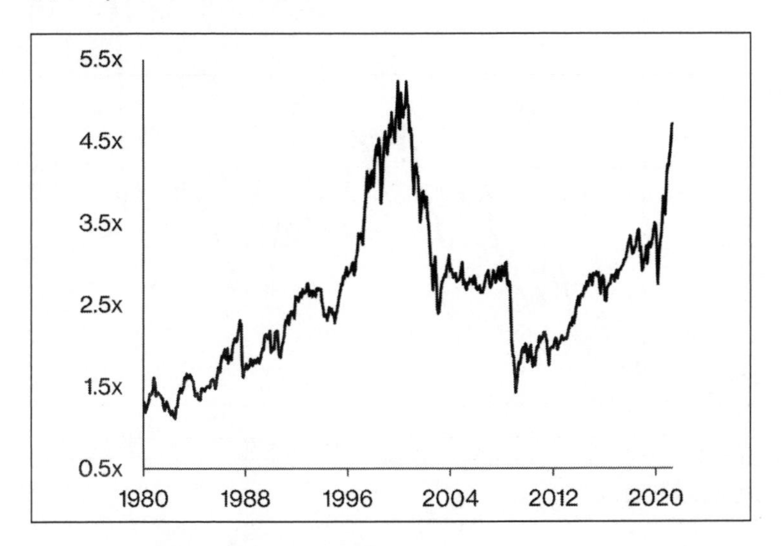

Source: Refinitiv Datastream, Federal Reserve

(b) US price-to-free cash flow ratio

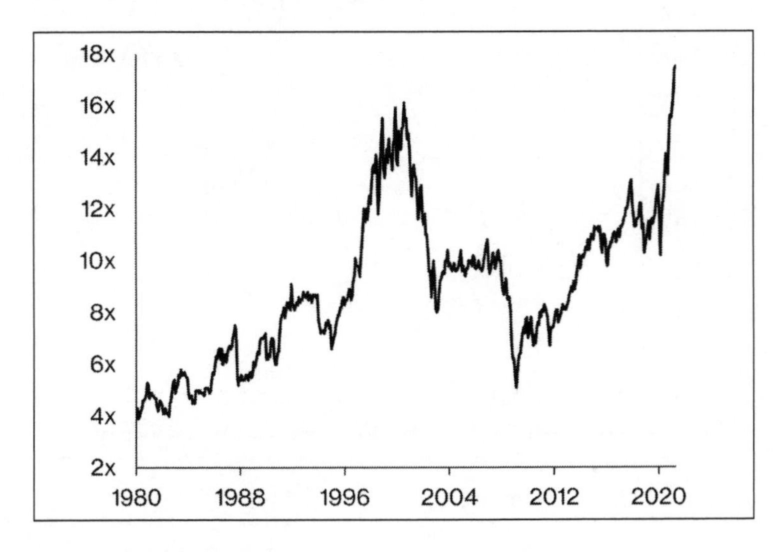

Source: Refinitiv Datastream

(c) US price/earnings ratio

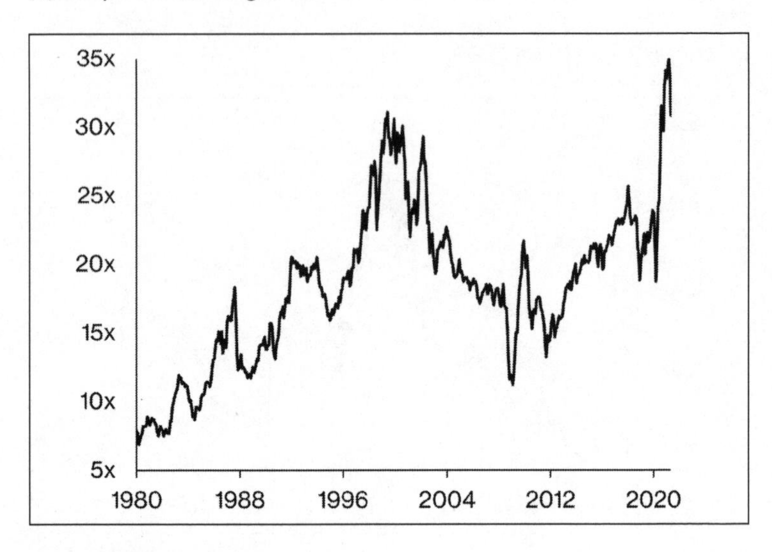

Source: Refinitiv Datastream

(d) Tobin Q – United States

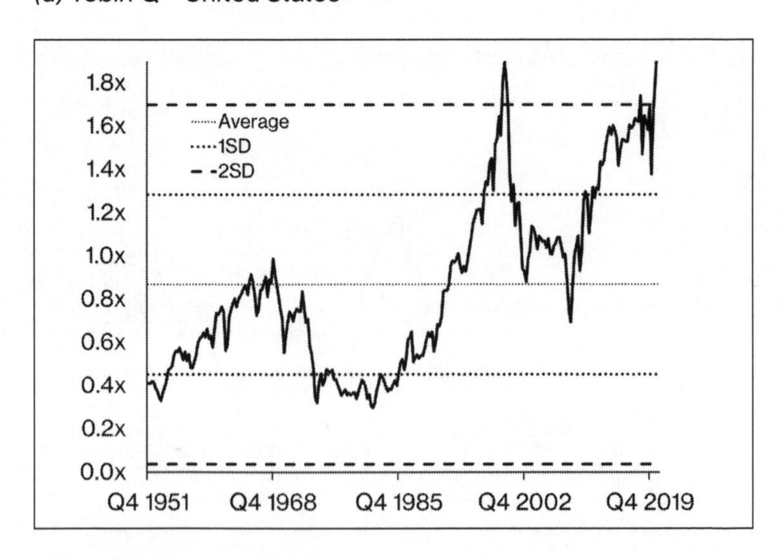

Source: Refinitiv Datastream

It is true that all individual metrics, by definition, only give a snapshot of how a market is being valued at a single point in time. That means the headline figures can be distorted by misleading short-term factors. For this reason, it is prudent and more helpful to use a measure which seeks to remove such distortions.

One popular measure of this kind is the cyclically adjusted price-to-earnings ratio (CAPE for short), designed by Professor Robert Shiller of Yale University. Strictly speaking, it is not cyclically adjusted, in the sense that the readings are adjusted for actual market and economic cycles. Rather it relies on using trailing ten-year average earnings as a proxy for the removal of cyclical factors when calculating the PE.

While a crude measure in that sense, it has the virtue of being both simple and having a long history that can be used to demonstrate its effectiveness as a guide to peaks and troughs in stock market performance. As figure 3 shows, the US CAPE valuation is at its second-highest level since modern stock market records began. This includes the 1929 peak. Just as importantly, it is currently more than two standard deviations above the historic average. The graph has been annotated to show the magnitudes of declines which followed each of the peaks. They do not make pleasant viewing.

The CAPE rating would only need to rise by 16% to become three standard deviations distant from the historic average. Past experience suggests this is a clear signal for investors to beware. It was not so long ago that market collapses were being attributed to 'three-standard-deviation' events (i.e., events having a probability of 0.3% or less) as an excuse for our inability to see them coming. More evocative than three-standard-deviation events were references to '1,000-year floods, although with recent climatic events this would perhaps carry somewhat less resonance.

Such arguments or references are typically deployed to suggest that the root cause is an unforecastable event, absolving those involved from blame for failing to anticipate the outcome. Another favourite metaphor is the so-called unforecastable 'black swan' event. The reality is that any mental model which has simply been defined using data from the wrong periods, or is based on false assumptions, will naturally fail to predict what comes next. A three-standard-deviation event in valuation is a classic warning sign, yet today it is being treated as a sideshow.

Figure 3: US cyclically-adjusted PE (1881–2021)

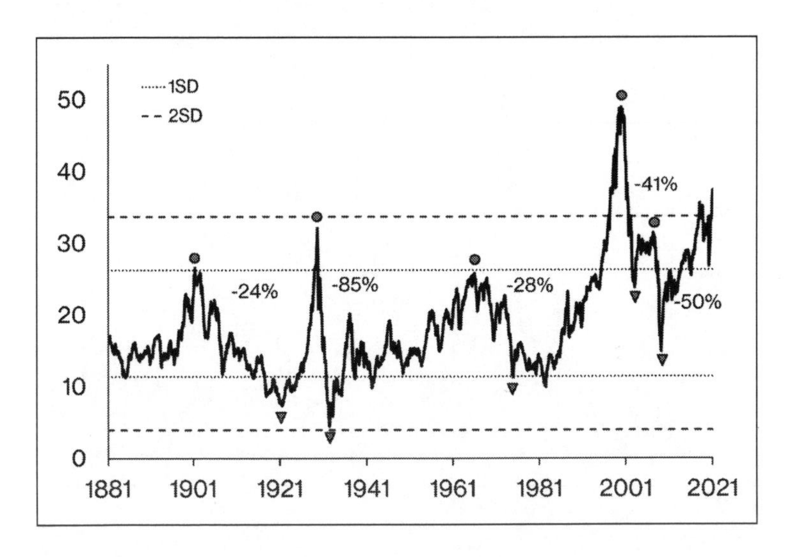

Source: Robert J. Shiller, econ.yale.edu, Refinitiv Datastream

Despite this apparent valuation anomaly, the great majority of investors and commentators are sanguine about the risk of markets coming down from their highs. This equanimity rests in part on a view that, although expensive on conventional measures, equities are not far out of line with historical experience when measured against the price of bonds.

Look, for example, at figure 4, which shows what Professor Shiller calls the 'excess equity yield', a measure that compares the earnings yield of companies in the stock market (their earnings as a percentage of their market capitalisation) to the ten-year US government bond yield.

Figure 4: Cyclically adjusted PE excess yield (1881–2021)

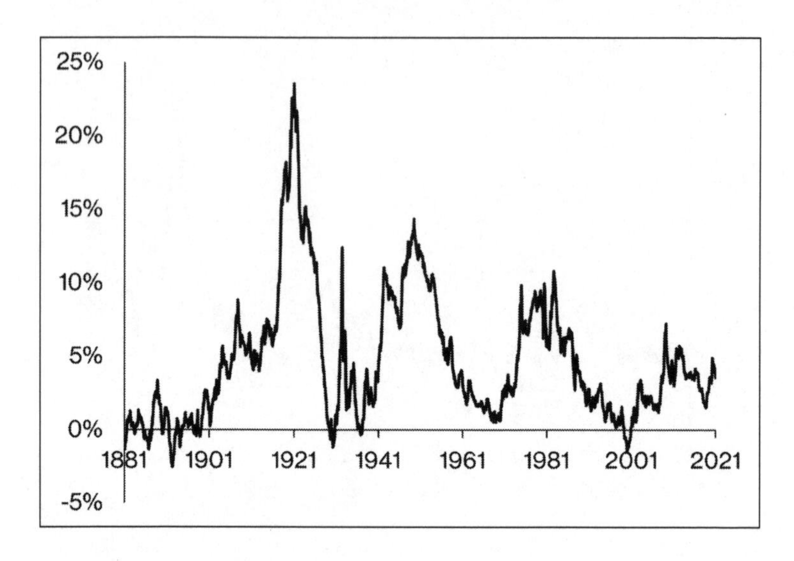

Source: Robert J. Shiller, econ.yale.edu

From this perspective, it is true that there does not appear to be too much to worry about. The current 'excess equity yield' appears somewhere in the middle of its historic range and is well below the levels that prevailed on this measure at the time of the great stock market crashes of 1929 and 2000.

If you are so minded, therefore, it is not that difficult to explain away the historically high CAPE by the fact that bond yields are currently the lowest they have been in the modern era. Whether it is wise to do so is another matter. A lot depends on whether or not you think that low bond yields are here to stay.

Bond markets

As figure 5 shows, it is certainly the case that headline nominal yields on bonds are extremely low and have been in long-term secular decline. Taking the yield on US Treasuries as the benchmark for movements in the cost of money, it is only too clear that interest rates have been on a declining trend ever since the early 1980s when Paul Volcker, the chairman of the Federal Reserve, was given a mandate to take decisive action to control the inflation that had devestated the global economy in the 1970s.

From a peak approaching 16%, the yield on the 10-year Treasury has declined to levels below 2% and until very recently appeared to be on track to fall below 0%, the so-called 'zero lower bound', something that has not been witnessed in modern times. There is no precedent for governments, even those with impeccable credit standing, being able to borrow money for anything but short periods at effectively no cost. It is not a sustainable state of affairs either in theory or in practice.

Yet in 2020, at the height of the markets' panicked reaction to the news that Covid-19 had become a global pandemic, the nominal yield on the 10-year Treasury fell to just 0.5%, while most Treasuries with shorter maturities traded in negative territory. They have since recovered, but bond yields remain very low by historical standards; the 10-year Treasury yield was around 1.5% in mid-June 2021.

This dramatic picture becomes even more unusual if you look at the metric which is of even greater concern to bond investors: the real (i.e., inflation-adjusted) yield they are being offered. Real yields are calculated by subtracting the rate of inflation from the nominal yield. Unless they are positive, which they normally are, those who buy the bonds and hold them to maturity are guaranteed to be worse off, after allowing for inflation, when their money is repaid than when they originally invested.

Since the global financial crisis there have been several periods when the real yields on many government bonds around the world have been negative, an almost unprecedented state of affairs. At one point in 2020, while the average nominal bond yield remained in positive teritory, more than a third of government debt around the globe was trading on a negative real yield, meaning that those who bought the debt, all other things being equal, would be guaranteed to see a gradual decline in their purchasing power.

Figure 5: US 10-year bond yields and inflation

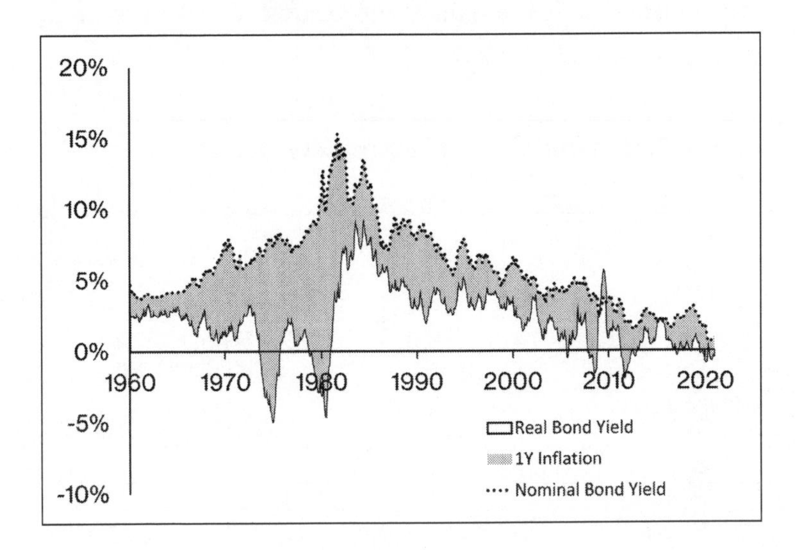

Source: Robert J. Shiller, econ.yale.edu

In fact, as figure 5 shows, real yields have been zero or below on several occasions since the global financial crisis. The last time this occurred was during the oil price crisis of the 1970s (not an encouraging precedent). Before that, the last time real yields were negative was after World War II, when, just like today, the authorities were deliberately suppressing interest rates to allow time for economic growth to return and help pay off the huge debts incurred in the war.

In both cases the inevitable outcome was large losses, both in nominal and real terms, for bond investors as the market eventually normalised. The problem for bond investors today is not only that bond yields at these very low levels mean that they provide next to no income, but that the risks of capital losses rise significantly at the same time. Only if bond yields remain at the same level or continue to fall can losses be avoided.

Figure 6: Nominal US bond and equity yields

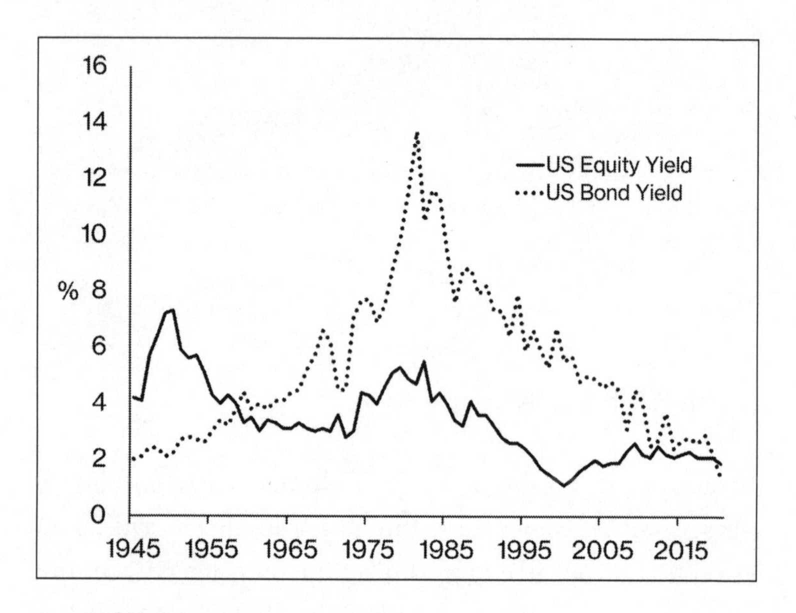

Source: Barclays Equity Gilt Study 2021

The obvious question to ask, then, is this: even if the high valuations being placed on stocks (and many other kinds of financial asset) are justified by the historically low cost of money, how sustainable are those current interest rates? If the argument is that the high price of stocks and many other assets is justified by such low bond yields, then logically those prices will not – and cannot – be sustained if and when yields start to rise.

The future for bonds

What explains this dramatic shift in the cost of money, and can it persist (as it needs to do to sustain asset prices where they are today)? Many explanations have been offered over the years. Mr Volcker's evident determination to eliminate inflation at whatever cost undoubtedly convinced a generation of professional investors that central banks could be relied upon to keep inflation under control.

Allied to that have been the powerful deflationary trends, mentioned above, that have helped drive inflation and future growth expectations lower across the world for the past 30 years. A combination of globalisation, demographic factors and technological advances have contributed to downward pressure on interest rates over a long period.

Another possible explanation lies in the changing relationship between savings and investment in the economy, which helps determine the market rate of interest. If there is a glut of savings, with too much money chasing too few investment opportunities, this could have the effect of keeping interest rates low.

This kind of analysis has been deployed by central bankers as an explanation for the persistent fall in interest rates.[7]

---

7 Minneapolisfed.org. 2021. Real Interest Rates over the Long Run | Federal Reserve Bank of Minneapolis. [online] Available at: www.minneapolisfed.org/article/2016/real-interest-rates-over-the-long-run

No less a figure than Ben Bernanke, then chairman of the Federal Reserve, argued in 2005 that a global savings glut helped to explain both the expansion of the US current account deficit and the low level of long-term real interest rates.[8]

In his view this too was one of the root causes of the global financial crisis, although that explanation does not square easily with the evidence of the widespread lending excesses that took place in the credit markets and which precipitated the sub-prime mortgage crisis, as graphically detailed by Michael Lewis in his book *The Big Short*.[9]

Why is this history important? The answer is that when asset prices are rising to new highs, as bond prices have continued to do over the last three decades, it is almost always possible to find some way to rationalise the outcome. These rationalisations tend to become more tortured as valuations rise and the signs of excess become more egregious.

This was just what we saw in the run up to the GFC, where so many obvious risks were ignored, subordinated to the view that either 'the market' was correct or, in the infamous words of the Citibank CEO Chuck Prince, everyone had an incentive to keep taking those risks:

---

8 Bernanke, B., 2005. Remarks by Governor Ben S. Bernanke, at the Sandridge Lecture, Virginia Association of Economists.

9 Lewis, M., 2010. *The Big Short: Inside the Doomsday Machine.* New York. W.W. Norton and Company.

> "When the music stops, in terms of liquidity, things will be complicated. But as long as the music is playing, you've got to get up and dance. We're still dancing."[10]

In other words, we know that investor behaviour can be driven as much by price action – the hard-to-resist temptation to join in a rising market – as by a rational view of the future and a calm assessment of the balance between risk and reward. It is a short step to go from saying that bond yields have kept on falling to convincing yourself that they must do so indefinitely, or at least as long as one's career prospects demand.

It is hard to avoid the conclusion that this process is exactly what we are seeing again today. Now that bond yields are so close to zero, there is clearly little room for the downward trend to persist, yet the markets appear to be priced on the assumption that the trend will never reverse. That view is at best complacent and at worst downright dangerous.

---

10 Nakamoto, M. and Wighton, D., 2007. Citigroup chief stays bullish on buy-outs. *Financial Times.*

3.
Risks and Speculation

A misguided policy response

THE EVIDENCE ALSO suggests that policymakers, for what are perhaps understandable reasons, have become complicit in promoting the view that the climate is ripe for taking risks. In the immediate aftermath of the global financial crisis, given the clear risk of a relapse into a 1930s-style implosion of the financial system, the purchase of the highest-quality bonds by central banks to sustain and guarantee liquidity in the bond market made perfect sense.

As the policy response evolved, however, this rationale has become less and less easy to defend. Unlike the 1930s, there has been no outbreak of Smoot-Hawley-type protectionism, nor any strangulation of liquidity by gold-standard-related exchange rates. Bank balance sheets have been recapitalised and in fact have rarely looked stronger. One of the primary aims of policy after 2008 was to allow the recapitalisation of the financial sector and avoid the bank failures which contributed to the Great Depression.

Figure 7: US banks' risk-based capital

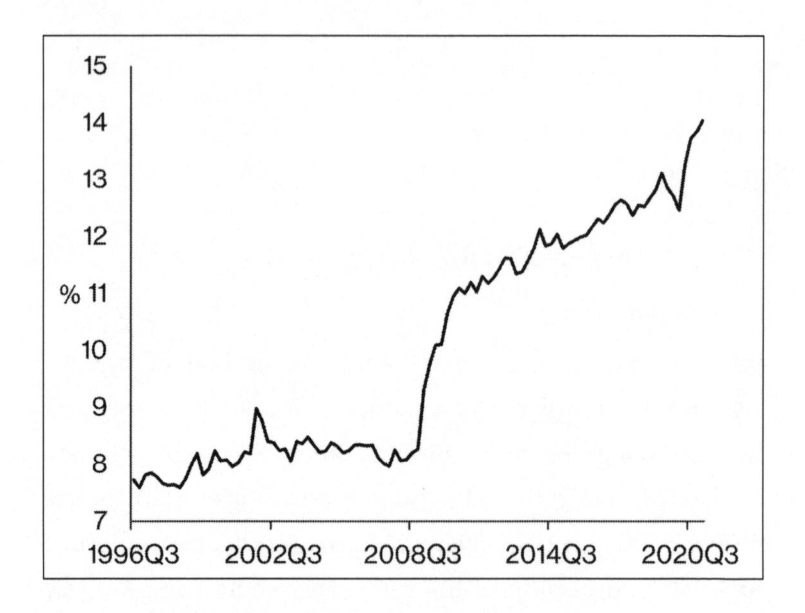

Source: FDIC Quarterly Banking Profile, 31 March 2021

Governments took direct stakes in banks to prevent their insolvency, whilst at the same time both increasing bank capital requirements and encouraging the rigorous write-off of poor loans. Using US banks as an example we can see just how successful this intervention has been. Figure 7 shows the risk-based capital of the major US banks relative to their total assets. This is the capital that banks need to hold back in order to cover operating losses in a severe downturn.

As can be seen from the chart, the capital ratios of US banks have improved from a figure of 8% in 2007 to nearly 14%. Yet repeated injections of liquidity and support for key financial institutions have continued long after the initial systemic threat has passed. Instead, as noted above, supporting the liqudity of the market has moved on to what now seems to have become an entrenched instrument of policy.

It provides the most obvious single explanation for the extreme elevation of asset prices we see today. Higher asset prices have become not just a happy consequence of monetary measures, but an explicitly articulated target of policymakers. For example, the Bank of England has this to say about QE on its website:

> "The aim of QE is simple: by creating this 'new' money, we aim to boost spending and investment in the economy … But there's a limit to how low interest rates can go. So, when we needed to act to boost the economy, we turned to another method of doing so: we introduced quantitative easing.
>
> "Large-scale purchases of government bonds lower the interest rates or 'yields' on those bonds. This pushes down on the interest rates offered on loans (e.g., mortgages or business loans) because rates on government bonds tend to affect other interest rates in the economy …
>
> "So, QE works by making it cheaper for households and businesses to borrow money – encouraging spending. In addition, QE can stimulate the economy by boosting a wide range of financial asset prices."[11]

---

11 'What is quantitative easing?' [online], Bankofengland.co.uk. Available at: www.bankofengland.co.uk/monetary-policy/quantitative-easing

The implicit guarantee that asset prices would be underpinned by central bank action has not been lost on financial markets. It was underlined in 2013 when, as conditions began to improve, the Federal Reserve's chairman Ben Bernanke signalled during testimony to Congress his intention to introduce a gradual phasing out, or tapering, of QE.

What followed was the so-called 'taper tantrum', the hostile and negative market reaction to the suggestion that the Federal Reserve's support could be phased out. Sufficiently rattled by the sharp market reaction, central banks reversed course and resumed their asset purchases.

Eight years later, not only is QE still with us, but the scale of the support has increased dramatically to much higher levels. At the time of the GFC the Federal Reserve carried around $1trn of debt on its balance sheet. Between 2008 and 2014 this doubled not once but twice. The scale and timing of these interventions is detailed in figure 8.

The first doubling can clearly be ascribed to the immediate support provided to keep the economy moving after the shock of the global financial crisis. The second doubling is less easy to attribute, other than as ongoing support to avoid asset price declines. QE was designed to be a temporary measure, but has turned out to be anything but. The final jump in debt, effectively the third doubling, was a direct response to the outbreak of the Covid-19 pandemic in 2020.

The current indications from the Federal Reserve are that 'support' will continue and this is evidenced in the continued expansion of the Fed balance sheet. Given that bank capital adequacy ratios have improved to the point that most banks are now overcapitalised, and Covid notwithstanding, it is hard to see the justification for continuing with QE for so long, unless targeting asset prices is at least part of the explanation.

The 'taper tantrum' surely provides one clue. Central banks, it seems, are still nervous about withdrawing financial support for fear of the potential market response, and in particular a sharp decline in asset prices. The political pressure to maintain the loose stance has been intense, widespread and shared by almost all parties across the political spectrum – so, as long as the bond markets remain complicit, there is little real incentive to change course.

Figure 8: Total assets, Federal Reserve

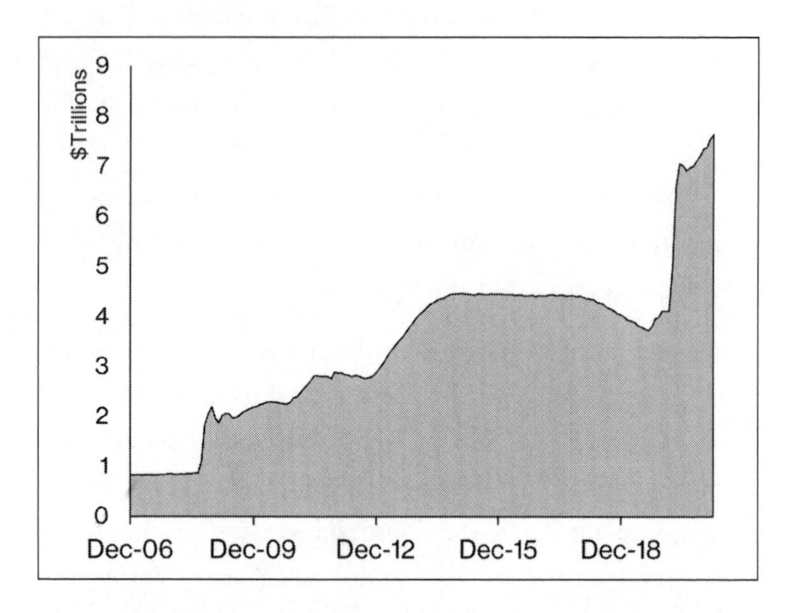

Source: Federal Reserve Bank, Recent Balance Sheet Trends, www.federalreserve.gov/monetarypolicy/bst_recenttrends.htm

The real question for bond investors is therefore how long in practice interest rates can remain at such historically low levels. Because it involves buying bonds and other assets in the market in vast amounts, QE has the effect of distorting the supply and demand equation. The Bank of England, for example, already owns around a third of the government bonds in issue, and there has to be a limit to how many more it can acquire.

Negative consequences

The huge bouts of monetary stimulus and prolonged suppression of interest rates are inevitably not without negative consequences. While we have experienced the short-term benefits of this unprecedented attempt to fix the market price of money, we have yet to feel the longer-term consequences. These are the ones to which prudent investors should be paying attention.

One side effect is that by holding down interest rates, QE has made it difficult for banks, despite their much healthier balance sheets, to make profitable new loans. The traditional banking model involves borrowing short and lending long, making a profit from the difference in interest rates. Those margins are not readily achievable in a distorted market without increasing the risk profile. This was precisely what happened prior to the GFC.

Another consequence weighing on central banks is the challenge of financing the rapidly expanding supply of debt being issued by governments. To take the US as an example: the outstanding Federal deficit was on a sharp upward trajectory even before the pandemic and has grown even more rapidly since. Outstanding US government debt at the end of 2020 stood at $27.7trn as compared with approximately $9.5trn at the beginning of 2008. The acceleration in debt since the GFC is clearly evident in figure 9.

Figure 9: Outstanding Federal debt

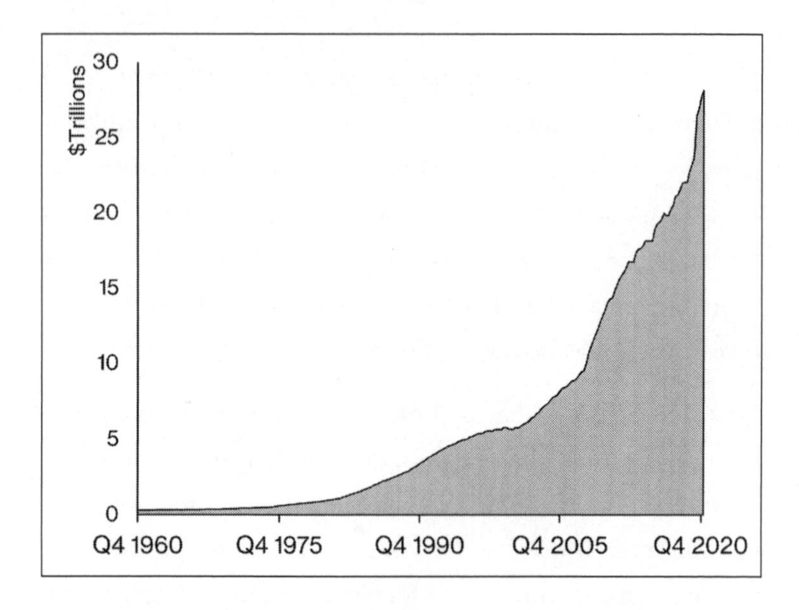

Source: Refinitiv Datastream, U.S. Department of the Treasury

Without the $7trn+ expansion of the Federal Reserve's balance sheet, the debt increase would have been much harder to finance and certainly impossible to do at such low current interest rates. The Biden administration is committed to further fiscal expansion, suggesting that the public debt burden could increase by a further 10% or even more. It is a similar story in many other developed economies.

The UK is a good example. The importance of QE in helping to fund the UK deficit is obvious. The economic history of the UK is one of periodic sterling crises as overseas investors react to the inflationary tendencies in the UK economy. The UK fiscal deficit can only be financed with some degree of external capital, which in turn requires competitive interest rates and a stable inflation outlook.

If you are relying on fiscal expansion to drive economic growth, there are obvious dangers if those conditions are not being met. Abandoning the insurance policy of underwriting asset markets through monetary stimulus would have severe consequences for future deficit funding. As Peter Warburton of Economic Perspectives notes, the Bank of England made little attempt to justify the £150bn of extra QE it announced in October 2020 on other grounds. The alignment of BoE gilt purchases and the public sector cash requirement shown in figure 10 is striking.

There is also another side effect to be considered. The gilts are purchased by the Bank of England using its Asset Purchase Facility (APF) and financed through the creation of additional central bank reserves which pay the policy rate, currently 0.1%. The gap between the policy rate and the yield payable on the gilts represents a net saving, estimated at £17.8bn for 2021–22.[12]

This saving comes at a cost of an effective reduction in the debt maturity and an increased sensitivity to interest-rate changes. To give a flavour of the orders of magnitude, if rates were 1% higher the impact on debt costs would increase debt interest spending by 0.8% of GDP. In other

12 obr.uk. 2021. *Debt maturity, quantitative easing and interest rate sensitivity.* [online] Available at: obr.uk/box/debt-maturity-quantitative-easing-and-interest-rate-sensitivity

words, even if the cost is not apparent, there is no free lunch with central bank funding of government debt.

Figure 10: BoE gilt purchases and public sector cash requirements

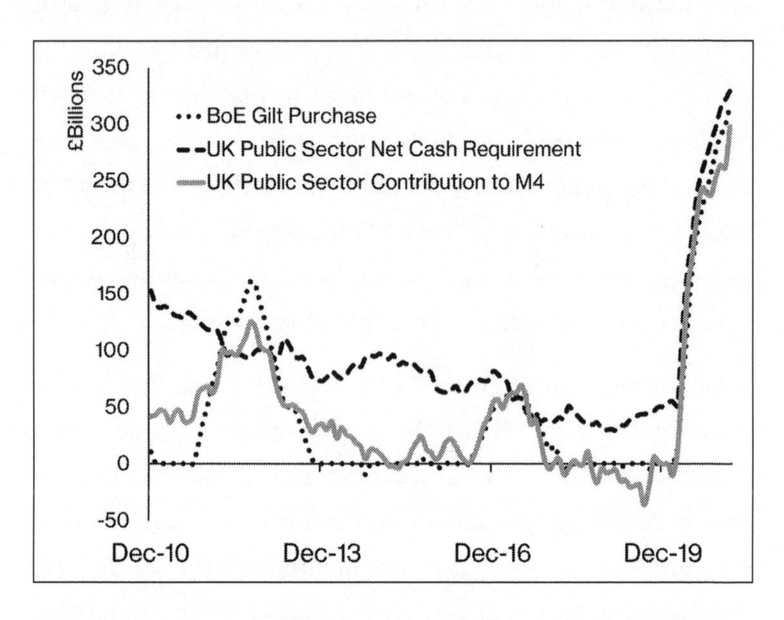

Source: Economic Perspectives, Refinitiv Datastream, Bank of England

The US and UK are not alone in pursuing expansionary fiscal policies. Fiscal expansion is now the conventional wisdom of all the major economies, as well as the key supranational bodies: the World Bank, the IMF and the OECD. The balance of advice is now all about supporting growth with government spending. Yet this comes against a backdrop where debt-to-GDP ratios in excess of 100% are already the norm rather than the exception.

How have we reached a stage where soaring debt is now so universal? Traditional monetarists believe that inflation is largely a monetary phenomenon. Yet we know that inflation in the conventional sense (as measured by retail or consumer price indices) has remained subdued throughout the 12 years since the GFC.

The answer to the sanguine attitude towards debt and monetary expansion lies in the inflation dog which has not barked. "At this stage, I think, nobody is very worried about debt," said Olivier Blanchard,[13] a senior fellow at the Peterson Institute for International Economics and a former chief economist for the IMF. "It's clear that we can probably go where we are going, which is debt ratios above 100% in many countries. And that's not the end of the world."

The risks in asset prices

There may not have been inflation in wages and consumer prices but the inflation in asset prices is obvious. The other consequence of low and falling bond yields has been dramatic increases in the prices of those bonds, and every other asset which is priced off the term structure of bond yields. There is no mystery about this. It is investment analysis 101.

---

13 Blanchard, O., 2020. August. *New York Times.*

For bondholders, the risks are obvious. Any increase in nominal yields will produce capital losses. The further interest rates fall, the more sensitive bond prices and their proxies become to changes in interest-rate expectations. What is odd about asset price inflation is that somehow it does not seem to carry the same negative connotation as wage- or producer-price inflation.

Asset inflation is hard to measure since one can always come up with an explanation as to why a particular asset is now worth more. Take 'risk-free' assets as an example. The US 10-year Treasury bond issued by the US government is the normal benchmark from which the pricing of many other assets is derived. What should the 10-year yield be?

Before the global financial crisis, investors typically demanded a minimum real yield of between 1% and 2%. If we merely assume that future inflation will run at 2%, which is the official target in most developed economies, then that implies looking for nominal yields in a range from 3% to 4%. Is the gap between the low current yield and this yield inflation or a bubble, and what happens if bond prices deflate?

That would not be the end of the world, as the IMF noted, but it would still imply a meaningful price correction. However, what if future inflation was suspected of moving to a sustainably higher trajectory? Not only would the nominal yield rise in response, but investors would certainly demand a higher real return as well. That is what historically has happened in such circumstances.

That would imply a real yield of at least the upper end of the 1-2% range might need to be added to whatever the new sustained inflation rate is. Simple arithmetic on assumptions of inflation in excess of 2% gives a minimum yield of 3%, and depending upon one's view of the likely new inflation rate potentially a range of 3–6%.

It is a simple matter to calculate the scale of the impact on bond prices if such a move were to happen. If the yield on the 10-year Treasury bond were to increase from 1.45% to 3%, the price, other things being equal, would have to fall by 13%. If this increase in yield also applied to the longer-dated 30-year bond, the price decline would exceed 30%.

By extension, if the yield were to rise to 6%, the impact on capital values would be considerably greater still. At the same time, on the basis that this would only happen if real yields were to return to positive territory, there would be significant losses also for owners of real assets such as index-linked bonds as well.

In reality the impact would spread to any assets which are effectively priced off the yield curve. Corporate bonds, real estate, works of art and classic cars, to name but a few, are all influenced by the prevailing rate of interest. The prices of all these assets will potentially suffer losses as well in the event of higher yields moving higher.

The suggestion that 10-year bond yields could even double to 3% might seem remote, given where we are today, but it is no more than what even a mild increase in inflationary expectations would entail. Such an outcome would have very serious consequences for both governments looking to fund their spending programmes and for anyone actively involved in the financial markets.

In particular, it would inflict heavy losses on those who have been ratcheting up their risk-taking in response to the conditions that easy-money policies have encouraged. When interest rates are kept below the natural market rate and credit is easy to find, it inevitably acts as a spur to higher leverage and greater risk-taking. That is how the seeds of most financial crises are sown.

Leverage and risk-taking

After more than ten years of continued yield suppression, it stretches credulity to believe that leverage and risk-taking in the private sector is not already contributing materially to the rise in asset prices. In fact, the signs of excess are observable not just in asset prices themselves, but also in the relaxation of lending standards and a lack of diligence with which new instruments and opportunities are being scrutinised.

Credit markets

The credit markets provide numerous examples of how income-seeking investors are taking greater risks in their search for higher yields. Five years ago, for example, the proportion of leveraged loans in the US rated B- or lower was under 10%.[14] It is now over one third of the outstanding amounts on loan. The CCC/CC/C category alone now accounts for more than 10% of the total.

The deterioration in the creditworthiness of outstanding debt is the result of both existing loans being downgraded to lower ratings and a fall in the quality of debt being issued. The share of CCC/CC/C debt in the total leveraged loan market is now back to the levels seen in the aftermath of the global financial crisis.

---

14 Bonds are rated on a scale, with AAA being the strongest rating, and all bonds rated lower than BBB- being collectively known as 'high yield' or 'junk bonds'.

Figure 11: Share of outstanding US leveraged loans, by S&P Global issuer rating

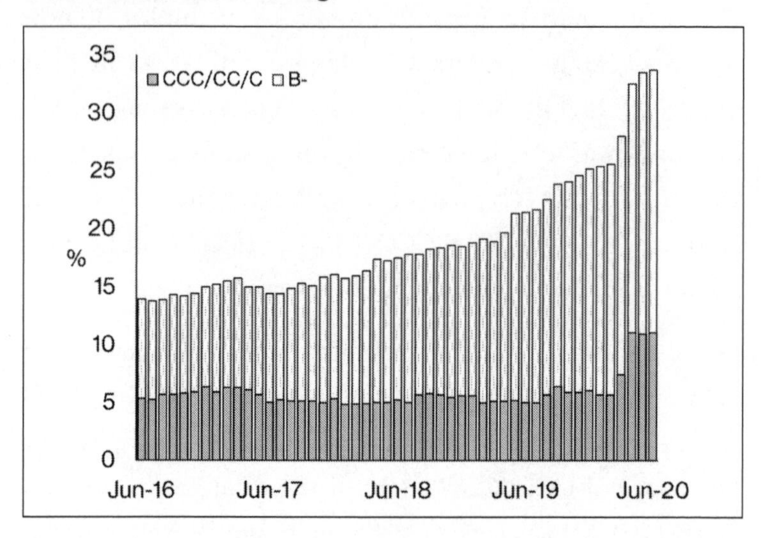

Source: LCD, an offering of S&P Global Market Intelligence; S&P/LSTA Leveraged Loan Index

Figure 12: Share of US leveraged loan issuers rated CCC/CC/C

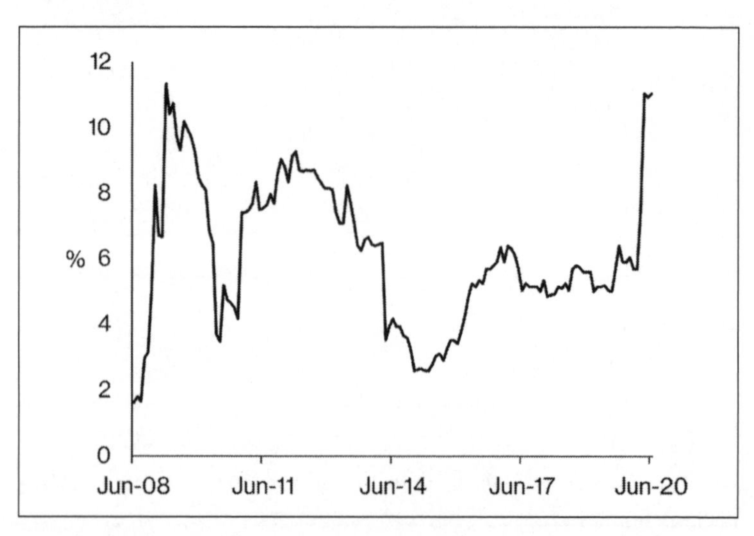

Source: LCD, an offering of S&P Global Market Intelligence; S&P/LSTA Leveraged Loan Index

Figure 13: Covenant-lite share of outstandings: US leveraged loans

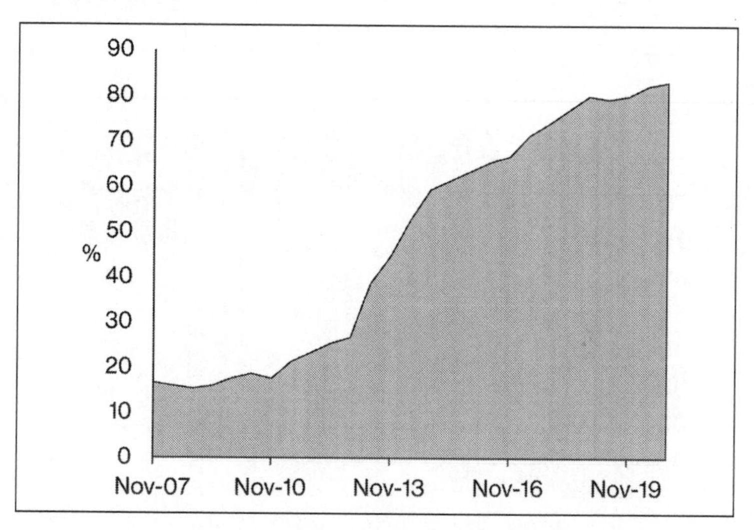

Source: LCD, an offering of S&P Global Market Intelligence

Turning to the quality of debt being issued, the increase in covenant-lite offerings (those without the normal protections to control risk within prudent parameters) is startling, having risen from under 20% at the time of the GFC to over 80% today (see figure 13).

As well as the absence of covenants, credit is being advanced on much laxer coverage ratios. The common multiple applied as a test is the ratio of debt to earnings before interest, tax and depreciation/amortisation. The availability of cash flow is critical to avoiding default – and the higher the ratio of debt to cash flow, the higher the commensurate risk.

Figure 14: Distribution of large institutional leveraged loan volumes, by debt-to-EBITDA ratio

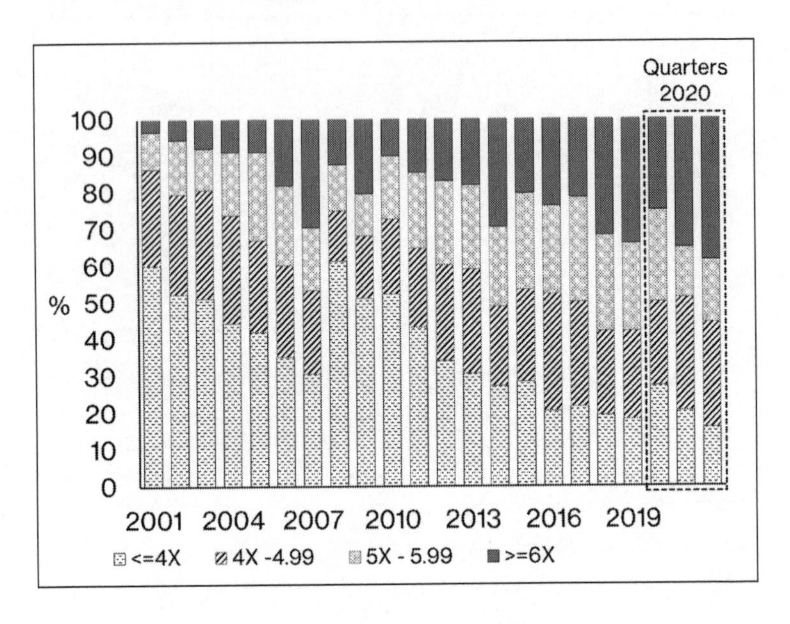

Source: S&P Global, Leveraged Commentary & Data

The chart clearly shows that lenders have become progressively more tolerant of lower cash flows. The quality of the cash flow has also deteriorated. Many borrowers have used creative techniques to massage the EBITDA number by adding back a range of items. This is normally a clear danger sign and one that has not been lost on the regulatory authorities, even if lenders seem more sanguine.

The *Financial Stability Report* of November 2018 from the Bank of England stated:

> "The scale, growth and deterioration of underwriting standards of leveraged lending in recent years share

similar trends with the US subprime mortgage market before the crisis."

Figure 15 details both the stated leverage and some estimates of what the true underlying leverage may be. It is unlikely that this will have become less of an issue from the time of the report to today.

Figure 15: Average leverage of global and UK issuers for new leveraged loans

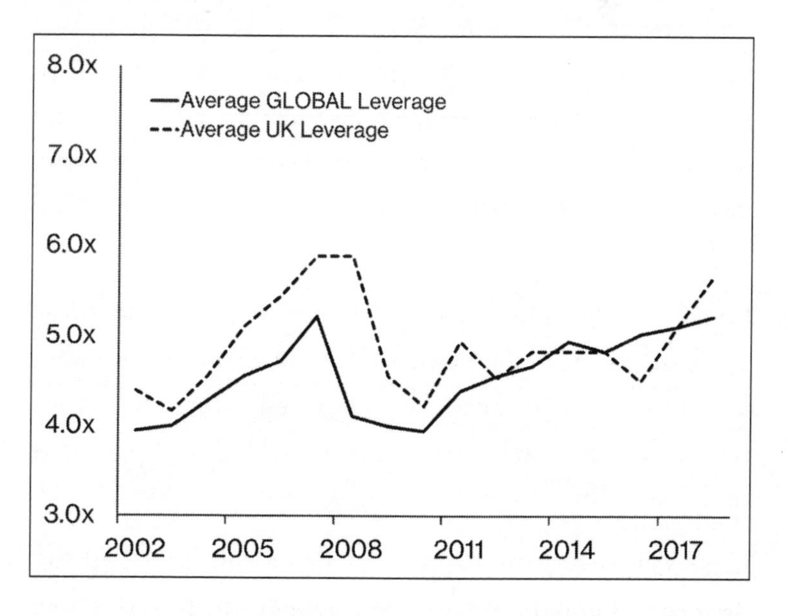

Source: *Financial Stability Report,* November 2018, issue no. 44, Covenant Review, LCD, S&P Global Market Intelligence and Bank calculations

The conclusion has to be that while QE was deployed as a tool to bring stability to financial markets and encourage investors to move out on the risk curve, it has become if anything too successful, in the sense of raising tolerance for risk well beyond normal prudential levels. The increase in risk is evident in the data: historic lows in yields, EBITDA gearing ratios higher than before the GFC, and covenant-lite borrowing dominating the leveraged loan sector.

It is important to remember that valuations of private debt and equity can be slow to react to changing circumstances. Given what we have already seen about valuation metrics deteriorating, it is highly likely that the full extent of problems in the debt markets will only be revealed when we have a sustained downturn. True, the banks are undoubtedly better positioned than they were ahead of the global financial crisis, but what we do know is that leverage and poor-quality lending have been occurring across the bank and non-bank debt markets.

Equities meanwhile, as noted earlier, are close to three standard deviations above their cyclically adjusted averages, and some stocks have been awarded such high price multiples that it would take decades of growth to bring them back down to normal ranges.

If the evidence from suppressed yields and increased risk were not enough, we can see similar frothiness across the investment spectrum. Thus far we have noted the increased issuance of higher-risk bonds and the low yields of the government securities of major economies. The ripple effect of these yields has spread to issuers whose history might have suggested that investor caution was the order of the day.

Sovereign bonds

Serial defaulters

In 2017, Argentina returned to the capital markets, raising a record-breaking $16bn. Investors shrugged off a history of eight previous sovereign defaults to snap up the bonds issued by the Macri government on the back of policies perceived as reform-oriented and market-friendly.

Such was the enthusiasm that investors approached the issuer seeking more supply. The outcome was the issue of a 100-year bond, sold on the view that, the more positive the view investors had, the longer the duration of instrument demanded. Not surprisingly, this positive view was partly fuelled by five years of buoyant bond and equity markets.

Figure 16: Argentine stocks and bonds

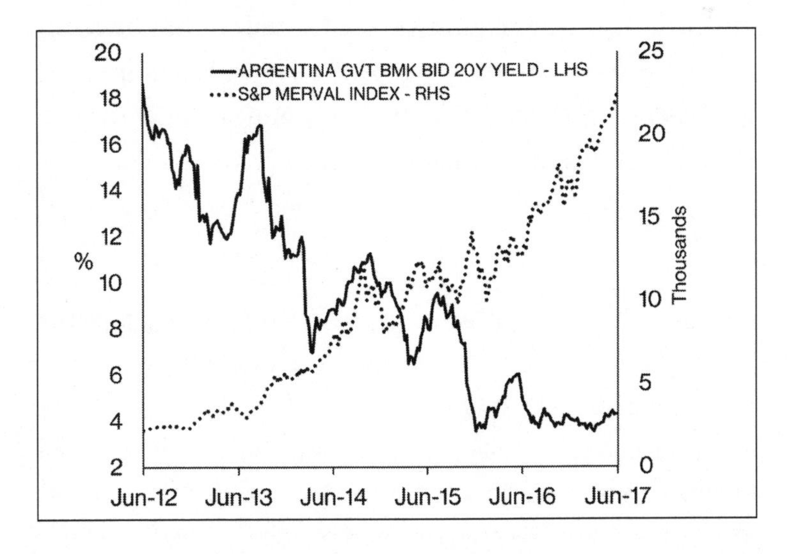

Source: Thomson Reuters Datastream, *Financial Times*

The coverage was the usual mixture of breathless enthusiasm and scepticism. The 'this time it's different' investors were banking that the "next 100 years will be very different than the last century", or that, in the near future, "few [were] expecting any major upsets".[15] The same article from which these quotes are drawn explicitly makes the point that this was "a risky bet that this time things were going to be different."

The *Financial Times* journalists who wrote that were reasonably prescient. Less than three years later the article title was 'Argentina heads for ninth sovereign debt default',[16] with the 100-year bond trading at just 26 cents on the dollar.

Beware of Greeks bearing gifts

The fiscal position of the Greek economy remains fragile, with debt-to-GDP in excess of 200%. There have been reforms, and the country's credit rating has recently improved to S&P BB from BB-. Notwithstanding the improvement, this classification still indicates debt which retains 'significant speculative characteristics'.

---

15 Mander, B. and Wrigglesworth, R., 2017. How did Argentina pull off a 100-year bond sale?. *Financial Times.* [online] Available at: www.ft.com/content/5ac33abc-551b-11e7-9fed-c19e2700005f

16 Mander, B. and Smith, C., 2020. Argentina heads for ninth sovereign debt default. *Financial Times.* [online] Available at: www.ft.com/content/2fab03a5-ed35-489e-8f24-980c488d1ec6

The question for investors is what return should be demanded for debt of this nature? The answer is none at all. The yield on Greek five-year debt has turned negative, apparently on the basis that the European Central Bank will continue to force down yields. As one investor stated: "You can't really position on sovereign spreads based on economic fundamentals. That's not what drives pricing."[17]

Figure 17: Negative Greek yields

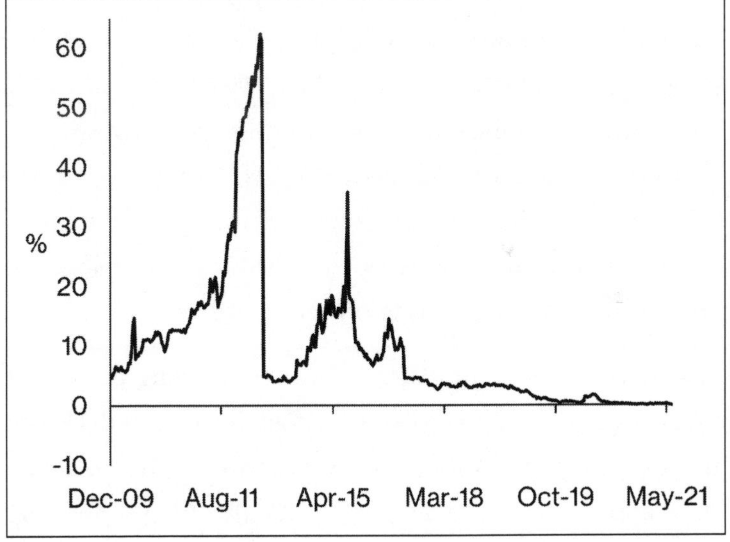

Source: Refinitiv, *Financial Times*

17 Stubbington, T., 2021. Greek 5-year bond yield turns negative for first time. *Financial Times.* [online] Available at: www.ft.com/content/db66bcb9-65d0-4671-a77f-928b88490fa2

Bond yields have continued to converge and there is little evidence of meaningful risk premia being attached to higher-risk issuers, even countries where the historical risks are well known and economic fragility self-evident. Instead, investors are being explicitly driven by a view that the central bank has their back, which removes any valuation anchor.

Meme stocks

Momentum trading involves purchasing (or selling) stocks which appear to have a clear price-direction trend. Those involved range from day-trading retail investors to sophisticated algorithmic hedge funds. It is based not on fundamental valuations but on pricing signals. Much of this revolves around purchasing on the back of accelerating price movement and exiting on the converse.

It is, in the investment lexicon, a game of 'being the fastest sheep' – and seeking to ensure you have exited before any downturn in price. The alternative is the so-called 'goat' approach, i.e., seeking out value by doing something different from the market and then holding the security until the value is recognised.

In 1841, Charles Mackay penned the classic book, *Extraordinary Popular Delusions and the Madness of Crowds,*[18] in

18 Mackay, C., 1850. *Extraordinary Popular Delusions and the Madness of Crowds.* Philadelphia: Lindsay and Blakiston.

which he explored examples of group irrationality ranging from the Crusades to alchemists, witches to stock market bubbles. This was an exposition of how groupthink (or the 'sheep') can combine to create outcomes which might otherwise seem so irrational as to never happen.

It is another way of stating the view expressed earlier that extrapolating a logical framework beyond what it can reasonably be expected to bear lies at the root of irrationality in asset prices.

In the modern world, social media looks like it might almost have been designed to support the creation of extraordinary popular delusions and stoke the madness of crowds. This is not lost on market participants, who can see the power of social media and its potential to create sharp price movements as everyone jumps on the latest bandwagon.

In this context, Reddit – a user-generated news-aggregation website – stands out. There have been multiple examples of 'Reddit meme stocks', where users have stimulated sufficient interest to dramatically shift the share price of individual stocks. When combined with technical support, the results can be explosive.

The most important technical position is stock liquidity. The less liquidity a stock has, the greater the price response to any purchases. The least liquid stocks are those where there is a significant outstanding short position on the stock. The reason for this is that for a stock to be shorted it has to be borrowed from the owner. Frequently this is done on margin, meaning that increased collateral is required if prices move in the wrong direction.

Shorting (or, in the language of the late 1800s, 'plunging') has a long history. The majority of short sellers operate on a short time horizon conditioned by technical factors. In some cases, detailed and extensive analysis has revealed fraud, corporate malfeasance or simply an inevitable path to business failure. The managements of such listed companies have sought to hide the facts from shareholders; the short sellers then seek to reveal them to the market.

Not surprisingly, short sellers who seek to expose corporate malfeasance are not well received by those whose (real or perceived) wrongs they seek to expose. It is a fairly small subset of the market, but these short sellers are typically thoughtful, forensic and patient. There is also a more nefarious subset – there are some short sellers who simply seek to spread rumours and hope for a market reaction. For companies under legitimate attack, the natural reaction is to try to categorise the thoughtful, forensic short-seller as one of the gambling rumour-mongers.

None of this is new. History is littered with examples of nefarious behaviour, with one of the most entertaining examples being the robber baron Jay Gould, who famously engineered a short squeeze on his erstwhile partner, Henry Smith, eliciting this exchange:

> "Smith, purple with rage, shoved his finger in Gould's face and sputtered, 'I will live to see the day, sir, when

> you have to earn a living by going around the street with a hand organ and a monkey.' 'Maybe you will, Henry, maybe you will,' Gould cooed softly. 'And when I want a monkey, Henry, I'll send for you.'"[19]

Things may have moved on from the days of the robber barons, but human nature remains unchanged. With the current negligible cost of money, we can expect leveraged high-risk activity to be prevalent. The modern environment is particularly perilous since we now have the power of social media to amplify speculation, the low cost of capital to fund it, and a diminished appreciation of risk fuelled by years of gains.

It is not a one-way street. Frothy markets combined with the social media echo chamber can also make shorting stocks potentially very dangerous. Consider a recent example which grabbed the headlines. GameStop Corporation is an operator of speciality game and PC entertainment stores. The move to direct sales and download rather than physical purchase has seen many equivalent businesses enter into terminal decline.

GameStop was showing similar characteristics, with revenue declines causing bottom-line losses. This attracted short sellers in the belief that, if the decline was not terminal, it certainly suggested a much lower value should be attributed to the business. Such was the negative consensus that at

---

19 Nairn, A., 2018. *Engines That Move Markets: Technology Investing from Railroads to the Internet and Beyond.* 2nd ed. Petersfield: Harriman House.

one point it appeared that the short position exceeded the available free float of the company shares.

Against this backdrop, all it took was sufficient positive movement in the share price to cause a panic. It is not clear whether the share price move was initiated on social media, but it was certainly amplified there. Squeezed short sellers were forced to cover their positions, frantically seeking out shares to purchase.

The share price continued to soar as social media participants, from YouTube viewers to Reddit users, jumped on the bandwagon. From a price of just under $20 it rose to nearly $350 at its peak, before returning to earth and then subsequently again rising.

This was a salutary lesson in the power of social media to initiate and propagate violent short-term share price movements. For the company, it provided an opportunity to raise capital at a price that would have been unthinkable just a few months earlier.

The power of social media evidenced in GameStop has been repeated with other stocks. This illusion of market power will continue to motivate investors and is likely to persist until the point when permanent losses in capital occur and act as a cold enough shower to dampen such animal spirits.

Figure 18: Gamestop

(a) Share price

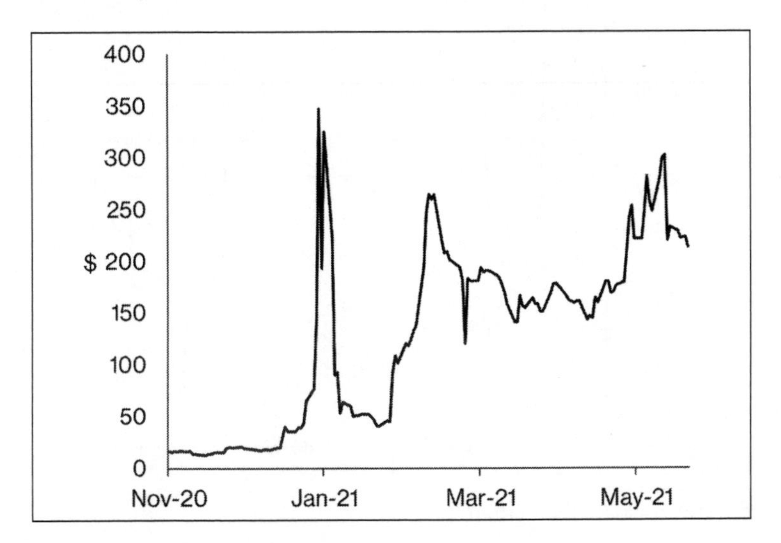

Source: Refinitiv Datastream

(b) Sales

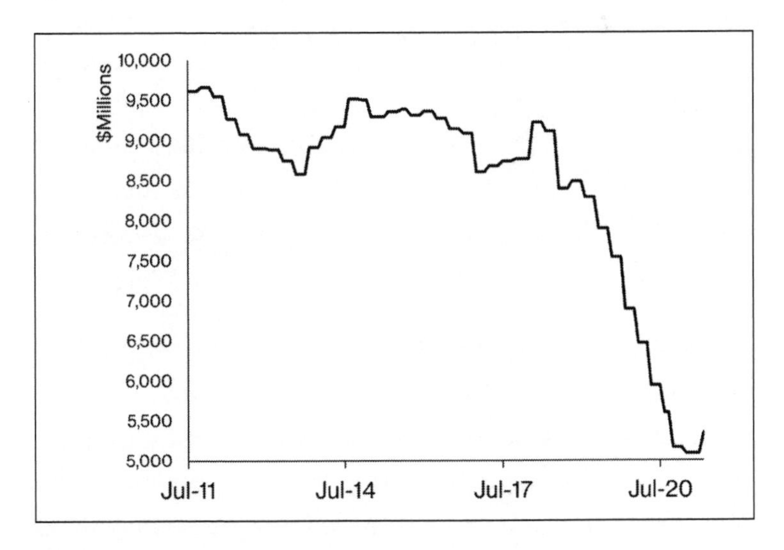

Source: Refinitiv Datastream

(c) Net profit

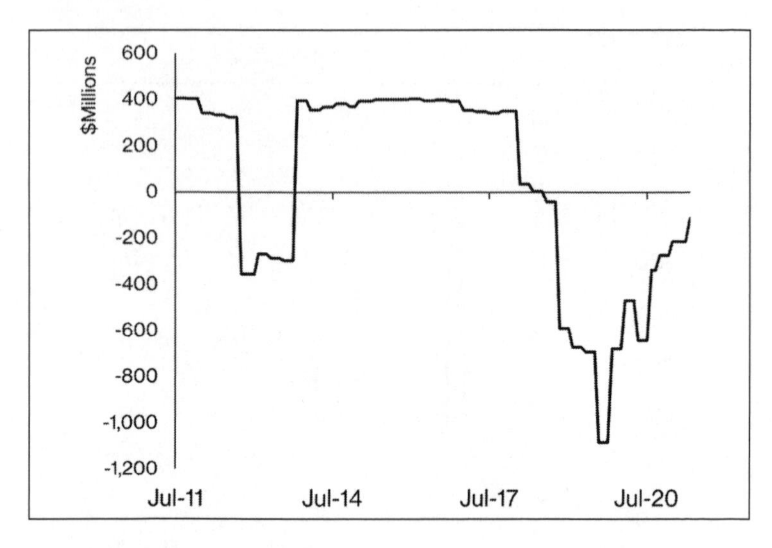

Source: Refinitiv Datastream

Special Purpose Acquisition Companies (SPACs)

If you wanted to design a structure to create an asymmetric risk profile for a group of investors, it would look something very much like a SPAC, the special purpose acquisition vehicles which have proliferated in the last two years.

In abstract, the concept seems a reasonable one. A group of investors launch an initial public offering (IPO) to raise capital from shareholders for a new special purpose company. Once a public listing has been obtained, the sponsors of the SPAC go out to find a private company to acquire and thus short-circuit the prolonged listing process that would be required if the target company was to seek an IPO itself.

In practice SPACs have a structure specifically designed for the benefit of the initial investors and sponsors, but which leaves the acquisition target – and any investors who later buy shares in the vehicle – with far inferior terms. The risk, in market parlance, is asymmetric: less risk for the originators and much more for everyone else. It is reminiscent of the incubator funds and listings of the TMT period, nearly all of which lost money for those who backed the original promoters on equally unfavourable terms.

The sponsor's edge comes from being able to claim additional equity in the SPAC after it has agreed an acquisition. The new shares are issued at a nominal price, termed the 'promote', and typically amount to 20% of the post-IPO equity. The sponsor also has the chance to gain from shares and warrants issued at the time of the IPO. Typically the sponsors have a period of two years in which to complete an acquisition or merger.

There is one other vital element of the SPAC. The initial shareholders have the right to redeem their shares for cash once an acquisition is completed. This capital has to be replaced by new funding, frequently in the form of private investments in public equity (PIPE for short). This creates additional dilution for the shareholders who remain.

SPACs are therefore exceptionally attractive for the initial sponsors and IPO investors, who can come in on very favourable terms and are frequently guaranteed an early exit. They are not a new phenomenon. Similar kinds of blind pool vehicles were in vogue during the South Sea Bubble and before the 1929 stock market crash, but they have grown rapidly in the last two years.

2020 saw SPACs raise $83bn in new capital and more than $97bn by March 2021 (*SPACInsider*). If this run rate was sustained, the annualised number would be over $320bn. Whilst the pace of issuance is unlikely to be sustained to reach this number, it does illustrate the potential for exponential growth. A full study on the returns for sponsors versus those for subsequent investors has been conducted by the European Corporate Governance Institute Working Paper 746/2021 if more information is required.

Figure 19: SPAC fundraising

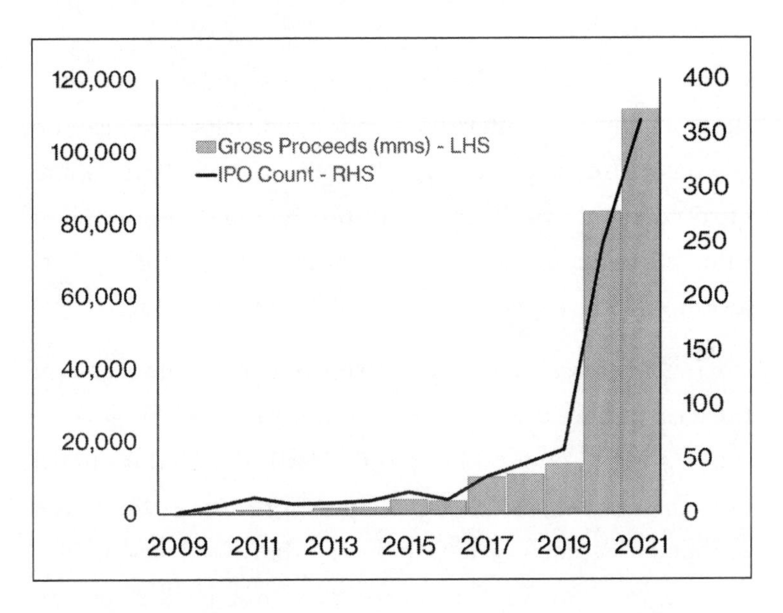

Note that 2021 is to end March which has already exceeded 2020 total
Source: SPACInsider

The point to note is that investors who accept such disadvantaged terms only do so if their appetite for risk is high. The SPAC phenomenon shows the degree to which valuation and risk have been subordinated to a belief that the market is only going one way – up. The same applies to those companies which agree to be acquired or merged by SPACs. They must believe that the heavily diluted outcome is better than what can be achieved by other methods, including a trade sale or a conventional IPO in their own name.

Cryptocurrencies

Cryptocurrencies like Bitcoin and Ethereum have increased dramatically in popularity in the last ten years. They can be seen as evidence of both growing distrust of conventional currencies in the face of unprecedented amounts of intervention, and the rise in speculative activity in markets awash with the liquidity provided by central banks.

Currencies have taken many forms over the centuries, but the last period when currencies were backed by gold or other physical commodities ended with the gold standard and the subsequent Great Depression. Since then, the monetary system has largely been what is termed a 'fiat' currency system. In this, currency is not backed by any physical commodity but is managed and backed by the nation's supervising power.

This is typically a country's central bank, which operates at various degrees of independence from the government. Faith in a particular currency therefore derives from the degree of confidence attached to the economy and government of the currency in question. Being well aware of this, governments regularly seek to sustain market confidence in their management of the economy and the operations of their central bank. Investors implicitly rely on the integrity and competence of the government in question.

For the central bank there is normally a mandate to manage monetary conditions in such a way as to achieve economic stability, frequently with some form of explicit inflation target. Cryptocurrencies are very different in their origins and purpose. In the words of Bitcoin's creator, Satoshi Nakamoto (a pseudonym for the still-anonymous creator of the digital currency), cryptocurrency is:

> "a purely peer-to-peer version of electronic cash … [allowing] online payments to be sent directly from one party to another without going through a financial institution … the network timestamps transactions by hashing them into an ongoing chain of hash-based proof-of-work … the longest chain not only serves as proof of the sequence of events witnessed, but proof that it came from the largest pool of CPU power."[20]

Rather than being printed or created by a nation's monetary authorities, as traditional currencies are, bitcoins are created by independent private sector agents known as 'miners'. Miners play the role of checking and updating transactions on the network when users send or receive bitcoins. This involves the use of high-powered computing to solve complex mathematics in the validation process. Valid transactions are recorded in a public log and miners are paid for this by the issue of new bitcoins.

---

20 Nakamoto, S., 2008. *Bitcoin: A Peer-to-Peer Electronic Cash System.* [ebook] Available at: https://bitcoin.org/bitcoin.pdf? [Accessed 15 June 2021].

This public log is called a 'distributed ledger' and the transactions are bundled up in blocks. When blocks are updated, they are added to the end of the ledger and contain a reference to the previous block, hence the term 'blockchain'. The blockchain makes cheating the system difficult, since to cheat would require greater computer power than the all the miners in aggregate already have. As the chains expand, the processing power required in the 'proof of work' phase also grows, which has led to serious concerns over the environmental impact of the level of energy consumption involved in the process.

The growth of the money supply is determined by the incentives paid to the miners who validate the blockchain. Crucially, the total supply of bitcoins is limited to 21m in the source code (or at least it is so stated). For many other cryptocurrencies the supply constraint is either less clear or non-existent. The investor has no legal national or supranational enforcement mechanism other than the simple law of contract. In other words, caveat emptor applies with full force.

Figure 20: Bitcoin closing price

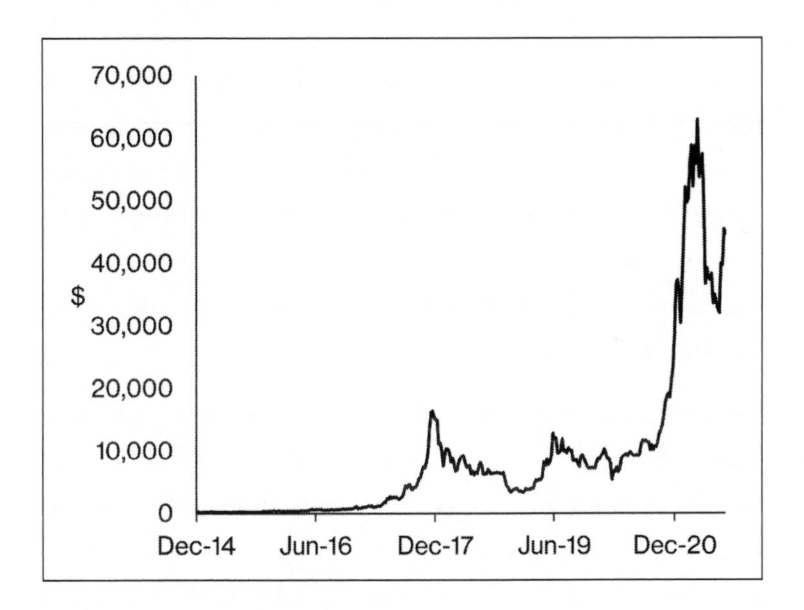

Source: Refinitiv Datastream

The rise in cryptocurrencies such as Bitcoin is due in part to the general frothiness of markets and in part to the rising fear of currency debasement. They can appeal to both speculators and risk-averse investors looking to hedge their exposure to potentially depreciating conventional currencies. Neither category, by definition, is demonstrating much faith in the underlying stability of the financial system.

Non-fungible tokens (NFTs)

In some ways NFTs are an extension of cryptocurrencies. Rather than taking the form of a currency, the blockchain methodology is attached to some form of unique digital property. Whilst an NFT is unique and can be bought and sold, it has no tangible form of its own. In this sense it is unlike owning an original work of art since the digital file can simply be duplicated.

There seems to be no limit to what has been sold and traded as NFTs, ranging from an alleged $2.5m for the first tweet made by Jack Dorsey, the founder of Twitter, to nearly $0.6m for the meme of a flying pop-art cat which, notwithstanding the sale, can still be distributed online.[21] In many cases the creator still retains the copyright. Perhaps it is no surprise that payments for such works are mostly made in cryptocurrency.

Recently an art NFT by Michael Winkelmann, the artist known as Beeple, was sold at a Christies auction for $69m. The artist then immediately converted the cryptocurrency payment into US dollars and commented, together with some much more colourful language, that the market was "absolutely a bubble".

---

21 www.nytimes.com. 2021. 'Why an Animated Flying Cat With a Pop-Tart Body Sold for Almost $600,000'.

Nothing new under the sun

There are echoes of famous past financial crises in the way that the financial markets have been driven up to new peaks. Consider this account of the market panic of 1893.

Panic of 1893

"The occurrence of the crisis, beginning in May, 1893, is well known.

Preceding indications – This preceding period is characterised by well-defined indications, some of which develop contemporaneously, but which, so far as they are distinct in time, occur in approximately the following order:

1. *An increase in prices, first, of special commodities, then, in a less degree, of commodities generally, and later of real estate, both improved and unimproved.*
2. *Increased activity of established enterprises, and the formation of many new ones, especially those which provide for increased production or improved methods, such as factories and furnaces, railways and ships, all requiring the change of circulating to fixed capital.*
3. *An active demand for loans at slightly higher rates of interest.*
4. *The general employment of labour at increasing or well-sustained wages.*
5. *Increasing extravagance in private and public expenditure.*

6. *The development of a mania for speculation, attended by dishonest methods in business and the gullibility of many investors.*
7. *Lastly, a great expansion of discounts and loans, and a resulting rise in the rate of interest; also a material increase in wages, attended by frequent strikes and by difficulty in obtaining a sufficient number of labourers to meet the demand.*

Many of the above tendencies are indications of genuine prosperity. They are precursors of disaster only in case of overaction, when the equipment for the creation of certain classes of commodities, and their consequent production, is out of harmony with that for other classes, and speculation takes the place of more legitimate enterprise.

It should be especially borne in mind that in the events preceding a crisis, as well as in any season of growing prosperity, the increase of activity as well as of prices is far from equal in different lines. Higher prices will first be quoted in some particular commodity or commodities, and later in the rest. The increase of activity and price is usually most noticeable in articles the production of which can most readily be enlarged or diminished by human volition, such as the so-called 'industrial elements' – coal, iron and steel, or timber; or in articles required to supply some new demand of convenience or luxury."[22]

22 Burton, T., 1902. *Financial Crises and Periods of Industrial and Commercial Depression.* New York: D Appleton & Co, chapter 3, pp.51–53.

Archegos Capital

In this context, the recent story regarding the collapse of Archegos Capital is an interesting warning of what may turn out to be other examples of excess, if and when credit conditions tighten. This was the family investment vehicle of Mr Hwang, a former hedge fund manager associated with Julian Robertson's Tiger Management business. In 2012, Mr Hwang and Tiger Asia were forced to settle criminal fraud charges of insider trading with a $44m settlement. Prevented from managing third-party money, Tiger Asia migrated to become Mr Hwang's family office.

In March 2021, Archegos had to liquidate its positions, creating substantial losses for its banks. Credit Suisse, for example, announced it would have to take a $4.7bn write-off. The root cause was that Archegos had taken big leveraged bets on a small number of companies. As the price of these companies fell, Mr Hwang was required either to sell the shares or provide more financing to the banks providing his credit. Given the leverage was allegedly as high as 20×, sale would have been the only option.

The point here is not just that the banks involved lost money, but that they were willing to supply the finance against trades where the high risk was obvious. This was not a case of a sophisticated layered strategy unravelling when some unexpected event occurred, more a case of staying on the dancefloor. It is impossible to believe that this will have been an isolated case. History suggests that leverage, encouraged by low interest rates, will be endemic through the system; or to quote from the above account of 1893:

> "The development of a mania for speculation, attended by dishonest methods in business and the gullibility of many investors."

Archegos may be only one of many early indicators of speculative excess ending in tears. According to one recent report,[23] 40% of individual investors are now trading with the help of leverage. Note that these are individuals, not hedge funds or family offices – where one can have a high degree of confidence that leverage will also have grown.

---

23 Wolff-Mann, E., 2020. *43% of retail investors are trading with leverage: survey*. [online] www.yahoo.com. Available at: https://finance.yahoo.com/news/43-of-retail-investors-are-trading-with-leverage-survey-172744302.html [Accessed 9 September 2020].

4.
Why Change is Coming

THE PREVIOUS SECTION does not make appetising reading for those seeking good returns from asset markets. In Sir John Templeton's words, the best time to invest is at the point of 'maximum pessimism'. This feels much more like a point of 'maximum optimism', one that ironically has been reinforced by the worst pandemic the modern world has seen. The signs of excess described earlier are difficult to interpret any other way.

Professional asset managers, however, are wired to seek out opportunities and as such typically have a built-in optimistic bias. They are also subconsciously wired to avoid career risk by straying too far from both their benchmark index and what their competitors are doing.

For most of the market cycle this is the correct approach to take. The market mechanism is remarkably resilient and has the ability to overcome seemingly impossible hurdles. That depends crucially, however, on the price signals in the market being fair and transparent and the rules of title and ownership being observed.

One of the reasons that the debt build-up which precipitated the GFC was able to progress as far as it did was because some participants in the financial system were able to hide the true levels of leverage they were taking on and misrepresent the underlying quality of their assets. The current context has similarities.

The suppression of interest rates has clearly achieved its goal of inflating asset prices. It is not just that asset prices have risen and appreciation of risk has diminished. If the cost of money is suppressed to zero, there are inevitable distributional effects. These apply to the population at large – and discussion of wealth distribution has become increasingly prominent.

There are also distributional effects within asset markets. Reduce the cost of debt and de-equitisation is encouraged, changing the structure of corporate balance sheets. Reduce the cost of debt and the 'risk-free' interest rate used to evaluate future cash flows diminishes, changing the value attached to more distant revenues. All of these distortions are evident today.

We won't know for sure until the markets retreat and we can find out where the problems are hidden, but it is highly likely that the underlying quality of many assets today is lower than stated. And when markets do retreat, questions will inevitably be asked about how far this excess of risk is the result of the deliberate manipulation of interest rates by central banks.

That the market has become addicted to the easy-money medicine which the authorities have been dispensing is clear. The addiction has been fuelled by central banks repeatedly revealing their fear of the consequences of a sustained asset market decline. It is not that the medicine was inappropriate when first prescribed, but rather that the markets should have been weaned off it earlier in order to prevent investors going 'cold turkey'.

The persistent intervention of the central banks means that the cost of money has not been set by the markets for well over a decade. This has not prevented policymakers, commentators and market participants such as Larry Summers regularly discussing the world as existing in "an era of low interest rates".[24] These commentators may not have meant that the era of low interest rates was natural and sustainable – but that is how it has been interpreted.

Once you define this era in the terms dictated by the central banks, it becomes much easier to draw conclusions which in any other era would have been seen as unsustainable or even irresponsible. Lord Macpherson, the former permanent secretary at the UK Treasury during the global financial crisis, points out, for example, that UK national debt will have spiralled from 27% of national income in 2001 to 110% by 2023.[25] He notes that if current negligible interest

24 Furman, J. and Summers, L., 2020. A Reconsideration of Fiscal Policy in the Era of Low Interest Rates.

25 McPherson, N., 2021. In defence of austerity. *Prospect.* [online] Available at: www.prospectmagazine.co.uk/author/nicholas-macpherson [Accessed 21 January 2021].

rates were to rise by just 2%, the incremental cost to the UK would be "over £50bn a year. The same as England spends each year on schools, squandered on servicing the debt."

It is legitimate to ask how the markets can have indulged this policy prescription for so long. After all, are not financial markets meant to price in all known information? The answer is that markets are not perfect in the sense that prices are always perfectly accurate. Repeated instances of market bubbles and crashes, and the existence of an active asset management industry, are evidence that accuracy is not always the outcome.

What happens in practice is that markets price different types of asset according to a perceived set of logical conditions. The logic works to a conclusion, but if the assumptions are wrong, so too will be the logical conclusions. At the times when markets are shown to have it got wrong, the explanation is often summed up by the use of terms such as 'new paradigm' or, in another favourite phrase of Sir John Templeton, the four most expensive words in the English language: 'this time it's different'.

The little brother of this phrase is 'you could have said the same thing last year', implying that because some predicted event has not happened within a prescribed period, it has become less likely to occur. That may be right if the logic or underlying assumptions are incorrect – but, if they are not, it clearly does not follow that an event has become less likely; indeed quite the contrary. What it does speak to is the tyranny of short-term comparisons to benchmarks and the dangers these hold in terms of career risk for investment professionals.

What happens on the investment case is that the elastic of stretched valuations stretches further as time elapses and the event becomes more likely, not less. The longer a misguided consensus assumption persists, in other words, the more likely it is to end badly.

Is this a new era?

The big question for investors is whether the warnings we have looked at so far add up to a reason for extreme investor caution, or whether this time it truly is different and the bull-market party can go on. As already noted, the consensus supporting current policy initiatives is widespread from supranational bodies such as the OECD and IMF through to national governments.

At the more extreme end we have the proponents of modern monetary theory (MMT), who see few limits to an expansionary role. Most of the precepts of MMT follow traditional economic theory; where they differ is in the MMT view that, since governments can issue sovereign currency, the only constraint is the availability of real resources and the inflationary consequences when such resources are fully utilised.

It is easy to see the politically seductive nature of this interpretation, given it ascribes a role to government in managing the economy to full employment. There are multiple critiques of the theoretical and practical issues with MMT, but the main point here is how the current environment has proved such fertile ground for its penetration of political thought.

Leaving aside MMT, the primary argument for the post-GFC policy consensus is rooted in the contention that not only have we moved into a new era of low interest rates, but that era is sustainable for many years. Three principal conclusions follow.

One is that, despite expansive use of QE and record low interest rates, there is little that monetary policy can do to raise the level of economic growth. Secondly, the new low-interest-rate regime implies that crowding out of private investment by massive government spending is unlikely. Finally, with interest rates at such levels, returns on spending and investment can plausibly be assumed to exceed funding costs – which allows those who accept this logic, crucially, to take a relaxed view of growing government indebtedness.

All these assumptions are dubious at best if the premise is incorrect. Earlier we noted the use of a 'savings glut' to explain the pre-GFC interest-rate regime and saving imbalances between the US and the developing world. It is notable that this explanation has been heard less often recently. It has been replaced with a tacit assumption that the downward trend in nominal and real interest rates initiated by Paul Volcker's assault on inflation back in the 1980s will persist.

But is the assumption that we are in a period of enduring low inflation and interest rates correct? It is true that charts show interest rates on a persistent downward trend since the Volcker era. However, it is important to note that there is a significant difference between the periods before and after the global financial crisis.

Before the GFC, ten-year bond yields averaged around 2% in real terms. It is only since the GFC that we have seen rates dip to zero or below. It is legitimate to argue that, in the early phases of the aftermath of the GFC period, a combination of investor concerns about the solvency of the financial system and a potential rerun of the 1930s deflationary slump drove the decline in yields.

However, that argument has become ever less plausible the longer the low-interest phenomenon has continued, given the way that the banking sector has been recapitalised and economic growth has resumed. It is frankly much more plausible that the explanation lies with the overt role played by central banks in seeking to suppress bond yields through their persistent policy intervention and stimulus, as outlined earlier.

Figure 21: Inflation and nominal bond rates of major economies

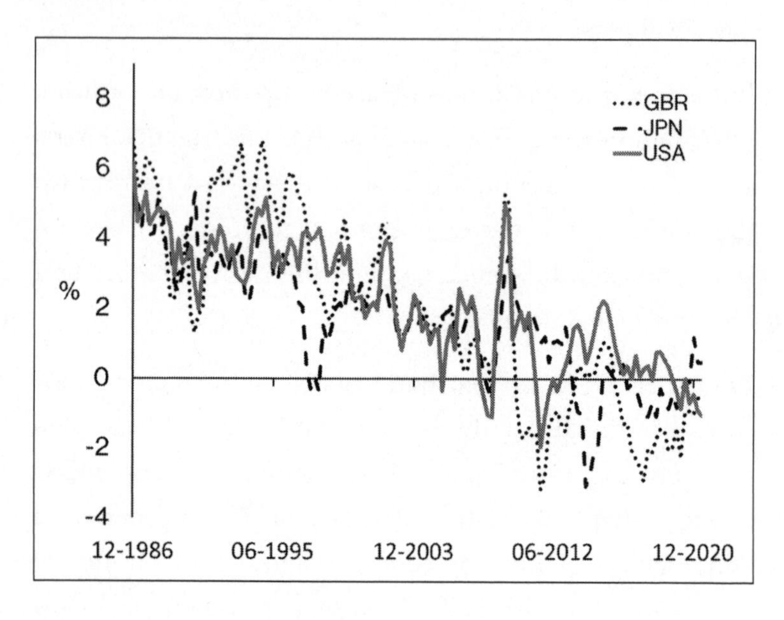

Source: Global Financial Data

Official forecasts not reliable

It is clear that the Federal Reserve and the current US administration are happy to encourage the new school of thought. Their projections paint a rosy picture of the future for interest rates, and in particular of the ability of the bond markets to absorb the unprecedented amounts of debt that have been and will continue to be issued to finance ballooning government deficits. Pragmatists are entitled, however, to take a more sceptical view of the numbers they present.

One reason is that official forecasts, while they provide valuable information, are not designed to give an unvarnished view of economic outlook. Forecasts are produced with a particular purpose and within certain binding constraints.

Central banks provide self-serving forward 'guidance' about the future path of policy in order to frame market expectations and reduce volatility. The Congressional Budget Office is required to base its long-term forecasts on the assumption of broadly unchanged tax and spending laws. You therefore need to consider their projections bearing in mind these constraints.

The Federal Reserve

The Federal Reserve's median economic forecasts for the next three years and beyond are detailed in table 1. If the forecasts are taken at face value, the Fed expects nominal growth of approximately 6% for the next two years and then 4.5% thereafter. Inflation meanwhile stays at the Fed's 2% target without there being any need to raise short rates until 2024. At that point they start to move towards 2.5%, which implies that around 0.5% is the approximately correct real interest rate at the short end.

Again, one has to remember that the document is part of the Federal Reserve's attempt to manage market expectations. In the current leveraged environment, from their perspective it would be extremely dangerous to do anything which might precipitate a market reaction and raise the cost of borrowing. It may be that the inflation forecast is genuinely what the Fed expects, but it is hard to believe that the Fed would put its name to a document at this juncture which included any above-target inflation forecast.

Table 1: Federal Reserve forecasts

Fed forecasts

Variable	2021	2022	2023	Longer term
Real GDP growth	4.2	3.2	2.4	1.8
Unemployment	5.0	4.2	3.7	4.1
PCE inflation	1.8	1.9	2.0	2.0
Projected appropriate policy path Fed Funds Rate	0.1	0.1	0.1	2.5

Source: Monetary Policy Report, 19 February 2021. Board of Governors of the Federal Reserve System.

It is notable, too, that the Fed has been increasingly talking about 'average' inflation rates and the possibility that in the short run the recovery might push rates above 2% without it having to intervene. This provides the central bank with considerable wiggle room, since the Fed explicitly acknowledges that "when inflation has been running persistently below 2%, appropriate monetary policy will likely aim to achieve inflation modestly above 2% for some time."[26]

The terms 'modestly' and 'some time' are carefully not defined, but the Fed explicitly highlights its willingness to ignore short-term deviations if they believe the longer-term path is still within their parameters. All of this falls squarely into the category of expectations management. The Fed is clearly well aware of the amount of leverage in the financial system and the fragility of credit. It knows that the threat of inflation pushing up the cost of credit could easily bring defaults and economic slowdown.

To be fair, it is entirely legitimate to discount some product and commodity price inflation when it is simply the arithmetic outcome of a rebound from the Covid-induced shock of 2020. If there were additional signs of inflationary pressures, it would be less legitimate for these to be discounted.

The official Fed projections assume that inflation will be well behaved and real economic growth settles at around 2% per annum. These forecasts will be touch points for asset markets. Should inflation come in significantly above the projected 'average' rate for a few months, the Fed will have to work hard to jawbone the markets to avoid a spike

---

26 federalreserve.gov. 2020. *Why does the Federal Reserve aim for inflation of 2 percent over the longer run?*. [online] Available at: www.federalreserve.gov/faqs/economy_14400.htm

in yields. Until now, the backdrop for Fed intervention has been a lagging economy. This would be different.

The same applies to evidence of strong real GDP growth. What, then, would be the supporting rationale for QE and interest-rate suppression if the economy were to boom? Once it became clear that the financial sector was not going to implode after the global financial crisis, all subsequent news was good news. Weak economic indicators implied more monetary-easing measures, which served to continue boosting asset prices. Strong economic news was received as vindication of policy and an underpinning for further asset-price advances.

It is entirely possible that we are now moving to an environment in which all news is bad news. Evidence of a strong economy in today's changed market conditions should imply less monetary and fiscal intervention. Less intervention implies the market may again determine the cost of money, with negative implications for asset prices.

On the other hand, an economy that weakens despite having the policy-tool sink thrown at it would suggest that there is not a fundamental underpinning for today's stratospheric valuations. In other words, the two-sided positive coin could be replaced by a negative version.

The Congressional Budget Office (CBO)

The CBO produces regular datasets and forecasts which provide helpful context on the implications for fiscal policy.

The requirement to assume unchanged tax and expenditure parameters makes the forecasts completely unrealistic as an expected outcome, but a helpful guide to what would happen to government debt given a change in economic outlook.

In its December 2020 publication,[27] the CBO provides a sensitivity analysis that shows the impact on debt interest payments of changes in the cost of funding, compared to the CBO's central case. The central case is, unsurprisingly, benign and reassuring for financial markets. It shows net interest as a percentage of GDP rising from 1.3% in 2010 to 1.6% this year, then remaining at this level until 2028, a further seven years out.

Table 2: CBO economic forecasts

CBO forecasts

Variable	2021	2022	2023	Longer term (2026–2031)
Real GDP growth	3.7	2.4	2.3	1.6
Unemployment	5.3	4.9	4.6	4.3
PCE inflation	1.7	1.9	1.9	2.1
Three-month Treasury bills	0.1	0.1	0.2	1.7
Ten-year Treasury notes	1.1	1.3	1.5	3.0

Source: An Overview of the Economic Outlook: 2021 to 2031, CBO, February 2021

27 Congressional Budget Office, 2020. *Federal Net Interest Costs: A Primer.*

The context here, we have to remember, is a debt position that has almost trebled in little more than ten years. The fallout from the GFC saw debt double from under $10trn to $20trn. After the response to the Covid pandemic has been paid for, assuming the measures currently being suggested are implemented, it is not difficult to see debt reaching $30trn. With such a level of debt to be financed, a benign outcome clearly rests heavily on assumptions about interest rates and projected tax revenues.

The CBO forecast assumes that the first half of the 2020s will see real growth in excess of 2% per annum, and nominal growth of 4%+ per annum once the exceptional recovery years of 2021 and 2022 are through. It is only in the latter part of the decade that real growth on the CBO figures falls below 2% and nominal growth continues around the 4% level. Thereafter, 20 years of uninterrupted moderate economic growth and inflation are posited. This is the economic backdrop for the projected tax revenue stream.

The cost of debt remains suppressed, with negative real yields forecast from 2020 to 2026, while nominal yields gradually creep up to 2% over the same period. In monetary terms the interest payment drops from $345bn in 2020 to a low of $272bn in 2023. As a percentage of GDP, debt-interest payments drop from 1.6% in 2020 to 1.2% in 2024, before gradually rising to nearly 2% by the end of the decade.

Too rosy a picture?

This is the kind of comfortable backdrop against which an expansive fiscal policy can be safely contemplated. However, the sensitivity of the debt-service burden to the expected level and shape of the yield curve is hugely important. The US, for example, has one of the shorter debt-maturity profiles amongst developed world countries at just over five years, and its debt carries an average weighted coupon of approximately 2%. (For reference, most developed economies average weighted maturities in the 5–8 year range, with the UK being the outlier at over 14 years.)

Also, as noted earlier, to the extent that debt has been funded by central banks there will have been a meaningful effective shortening in the maturity and a corresponding increase in the immediacy of the impact on funding costs. The maturity profile is important since it explains how, despite a massive increase in its debt burden, the projected interest payments the US has to make *fall* rather than increase until 2025 on the CBO forecasts.

Put simply, expensive debt is being refinanced at cheaper rates. It is not unreasonable therefore to assume that net interest payment will decline if interest-rate assumptions are correct, but it also means that sensitivity to rising rates grows commensurately. The magnitude of what is unfolding is captured in figures 22 and 23. These charts show the CBO budgetary projections based on the existing fiscal framework.

Federal debt expands from its current historic pandemic peak to almost double that level of 200% of GDP. As a consequence, the annual fiscal deficit eventually becomes dominated by interest costs, so that to achieve a fiscal balance a primary surplus in excess of 5% of GDP would be required. Just for context, this is similar to the much-derided fiscal debt position in Italy. The world is well aware of the political and economic difficulty of escaping from a position where a primary surplus alone brings little respite to the accumulated debt overhang.

Figure 22: CBO forecast US debt as % of GDP

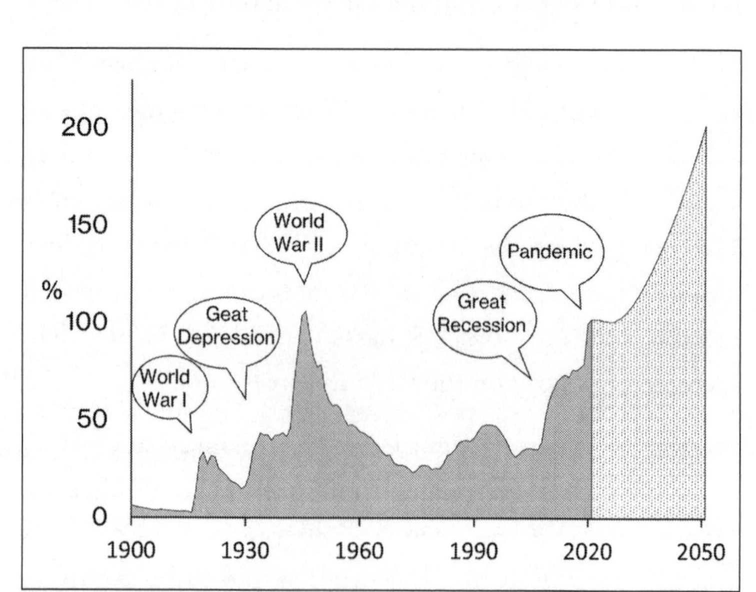

Source: CBO. www.cbo.gov/publication/56977#data

Figure 23: Annual deficit: primary and interest cost

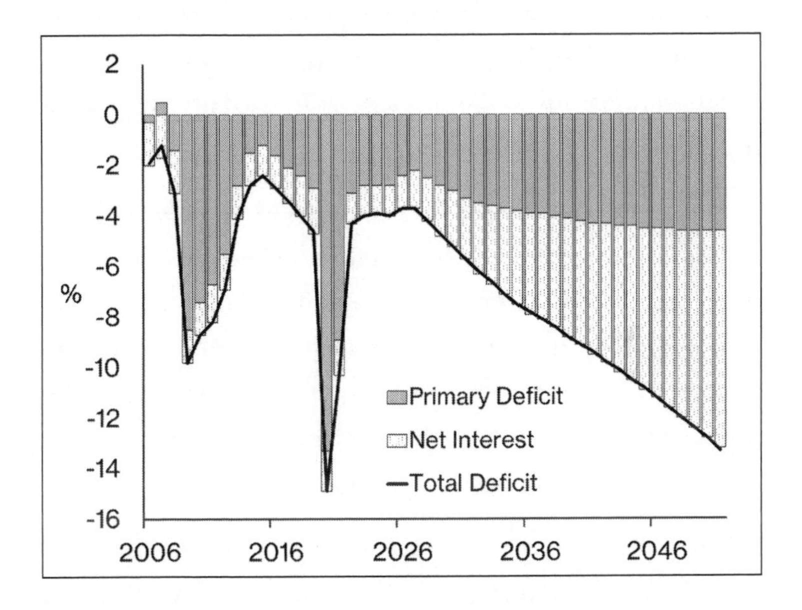

Source: CBO. www.cbo.gov/publication/56977#data

If the debt position were not bad enough, the projected out-turn could be much worse. The CBO graphs detailed above are predicated on benign interest rate assumptions. For example, the CBO estimates that every 10bp annual increase in rates would increase the Treasury's interest payments by $18bn a year in 2022, and by as much as $71bn in 2025. The impact of a 100bp rise in rates is therefore highly significant.

Such a rise in rates would more than double the interest burden to be met in 2023 and nearly triple it in 2025. Just to put this latter figure into context, it would mean that interest payments alone would account for over 3.5% of

GDP. This outcome is not an outlandish proposition. A 100bp increase in the US ten-year yield would still leave the real yield well below historic averages, assuming current inflation rates, and still imply a negative real interest rate at the short end of the yield curve.

To put this the other way round, the benign outlook which underpins projected fiscal projections will not be sustainable if real interest rates were to return to their normal historical range. If inflation were to spike, for example, and the market reacted by pushing up nominal yields in compensation, the implications for funding the debt burden would present extremely difficult political questions.

If it is right to be sceptical about current official forecasts for the next few years, scepticism turns to incredulity if you start to look at numbers out to the longer horizon of 2050. The CBO suggests that by 2050 the budget deficit will approach 200% of GDP, with a primary deficit of over 4% and interest costs of 6.5% of GDP – and this is based on a benign economic environment. Of all potential outcomes, we know that this is one that will not happen.

Of course, it can be argued that the short-term forecasts of both the Fed and the CBO for economic growth are likely to prove conservative, given the extent of planned fiscal pump priming and the scope for a stronger-than-expected or more rapid recovery from the pandemic. If the world turns out the way that the CBO projects, it is possible that, in the short run, asset markets could sustain their current levels.

The hunt for yield would continue, given a backdrop of gently rising inflation and reasonably robust nominal and real growth. The problem is that the backdrop for all of this is a singularly uninviting longer-term picture which has hitherto been ignored, but is now looming large.

Government intervention moving centre stage

The tide in political thought towards greater state intervention has been gathering pace for some considerable time. Both public opinion and the markets appear to support governments embarking on ever more fiscal initiatives. While the preferred instruments of intervention vary from one political party to the next, plans to increase debt and suppress interest rates are common to them all. While they may pay lip service to the idea of debt sustainability, fiscal restraint is nowhere on the cards. Austerity has become a dirty word.

The justification for this fiscal largesse derives from the idea floated by Jason Furman and Lawrence Summers that fiscal expansion will be self-financing, thanks to the returns it will generate being greater than the funding cost. There are echoes here of the Laffer-curve arguments favoured on the right of the political spectrum. (The argument that tax cuts can be self-funding because they provide incentives for entrepreneurship and growth.)

The problem is that, once adopted by gung-ho politicians, these ideas tend to quickly be taken to extremes that dangerously distort other parts of the economic system, with damaging consequences. Even those who advocate more fiscal action are beginning to voice concern about the need to ensure that fiscal injections are carefully measured and calibrated.

In a recent *FT* interview,[28] exactly these points were made by Summers, even though he is not someone who is ideologically opposed to increased government intervention.

What needs to be realised, however, is that the momentum behind the move towards 'more government' as the solution is now sufficiently well entrenched that it will not be reversed until the negative consequences become obvious and start to impact everyday life. In some ways it is reminiscent of the move towards 'free' markets in the Anglo-Saxon economies under Ronald Reagan and Margaret Thatcher.

Such was the economic mess at that time that a consensus emerged that something had to be done to redeem the situation, even knowing that the side effects would be unpleasant. In the UK, for example, this was a period of rapid inflation, government-determined 'price and

---

28 Wolf, M., 2021. Larry Summers: 'I'm concerned that what is being done is substantially excessive'. *Financial Times.* [online] Available at: www.ft.com/content/380ea811-e927-4fe1-aa5b-d213816e9073 [Accessed 12 April 2021].

income' policies and severe labour unrest underpinned by the collective wage-bargaining process. Support for the remedial policies remained for an extended period and probably beyond the point where they had moved from being economically determined to being more doctrinaire in nature.

The current environment is similar, except that the pendulum of public opinion has swung in the opposite direction There is a growing consensus that markets have failed to deliver socially acceptable outcomes and that rewards have flowed mainly to a small subset of the population. Allied to this is a recognition that governments have so far successfully mitigated the after-effects of the GFC without igniting inflation.

Indeed, if there is a public criticism of policy, it is that intervention should have been larger and more sustained. The apparent acquiescence of markets to the leap in debt arising from the policy response to the pandemic has reinforced the support for active government intervention.

As a consequence, while the global financial crisis was followed by a period during which there was an attempt to reduce government debt ratios back to historic levels, the new orthodoxy is that this is neither necessary nor appropriate. The idea of austerity has lost all credibility. While the path of debt outlined by bodies such as the CBO points to the need for tax rises, the reaction of governments is more likely to be: 'make me virtuous, but not yet'. The trend, in other words, will not be easily reversed.

Politically viable taxes

The first measure, nevertheless, *is* likely to be tax rises – at least those of a politically acceptable nature. This will not come as a surprise. In the United States, much of this was presaged during the last presidential election and in subsequent public announcements. Thus far the market reaction has been positive, as the pre-election promises enter the post-election posturing and haggling process. To the extent that debt levels require revenue raising, posturing will move to action and any market fears of interest rises will only accelerate this.

Some tax increases look inevitable, the question being which are the most politically acceptable. The obvious starting point will be to target those groups which appear to be either avoiding their 'fair share' of tax, or 'unfairly' benefitting from the current environment. In the first category will fall many companies that have used the freedom conferred by the reduced need for fixed assets to produce earnings growth and place intangible assets in low-tax zones. Expect robust action and a publicity campaign that highlights abuses of the international tax system.

This will be led by the US because of the extra-territorial power that is conferred by having reserve currency status through the banking system. The major developed countries will fall in behind, and whilst tax planners will soon be busy devising countermeasures, we can still expect effective tax rates to rise for those involved. The publicity campaign will not just involve more aggressive implementation of the existing tax code but focus on potential monopoly infringements.

As the numbers mentioned earlier illustrate, the funding deficit gap post-pandemic simply cannot be closed without tax rises, and corporate taxes carry few political costs. The technology sector is already threatened by government action against monopoly abuses and will find few unpaid friends to defend their use of tax havens to reduce their effective tax rates. Public statements which take the form of 'we pay all the taxes we are legally required to pay' are true as far as they go, but nevertheless disingenuous. What is legally required is likely to change. The move in this direction is already evident.

We can also expect the tax system to become less regressive. Whether it takes the form of higher marginal rates for the wealthiest, removal of tax exemptions or explicit taxes on wealth, it will be politically necessary to attack this group. One reason is the need for a smokescreen to hide the fact that meaningful increases in tax revenue are impossible without increasing the burden on the majority of the population.

Explaining why 'those with the broadest shoulders' should be contributing more will not be a difficult argument to sustain, given the relative advantages that have been conferred on the biggest earners in recent years. The increased proportion of rewards flowing to a narrower section of society can be seen in the Gini coefficient shown in figure 24. (The Gini coefficient is a measure of the gap between a completely equal distribution of incomes in an economy and the actual out-turn. A coefficient of 0 occurs when the distribution of incomes is completely equal and a coefficient of 1 results when one household has all the income.)

Figure 24: US total Gini coefficient

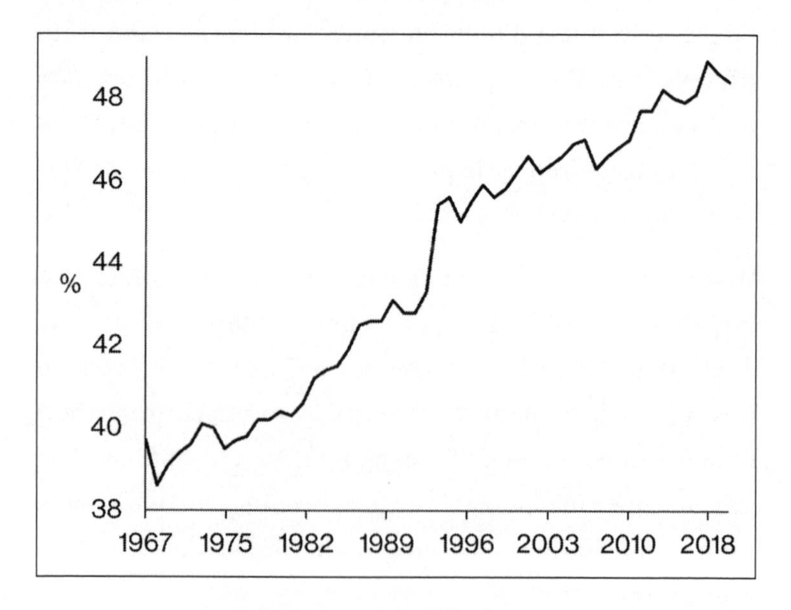

Source: Refinitiv Datastream, U.S. Census Bureau

The third area where tax rises seem inevitable will be to help pay for the 'green' agenda. The argument that the producers of pollution have rarely been forced to bear the cost of their negative externalities is clearly correct. The move towards a low-carbon world will not come cheap and what better way than to level the playing field by raising revenues from the polluters? The mother of all lobbying battles will play out in political capitals.

All of these likely tax policies will impose higher costs on businesses and lower their after-tax profits, which until the pandemic hit were running at record-high levels. In the worst case, shareholders will suffer the double whammy of lower profits cutting market valuations, while also facing the prospect of higher taxes on both income and capital gains. Even if higher taxes serve to reduce future government funding requirements, it is another reason for being cautious about future returns from the equity market.

5.

Is Economic Growth the Answer?

DURING MY PHD studies, one of my supervisors liked to quote a well-known axiom that, "whilst the spoken word is oft forgot, the written word stands to condemn". It was intended as a cautionary note emphasising that great care is needed when setting out written arguments. In academia, such care often produces conclusions that are caveated to the point of tediousness. In the real world of investment, it is not just the written word that may be an issue: the spoken word can also condemn.

In 1929 the renowned neoclassical economist and investor Irving Fisher made a speech to the Purchasing Agents Association at the Builders Exchange Club in New York, subsequently quoted in the *New York Times* on 16 October 1929. He unwisely offered the opinion that stock prices had reached "what looks like a permanently high plateau". Another well-known market participant, Roger Babson, was meanwhile warning[29] of the opposite outcome, that "sooner or later a crash is coming, and it may be terrific".

---

29 Galbraith, J., 1954. *The Great Crash.* New York: Penguin.

On the eve of the 1929 crash it was therefore possible to find eminent and thoughtful protagonists on both sides of the valuation debate. Today we might not have quite had the sixfold increase in the Dow Jones Industrial Average which was seen in the Roaring Twenties, but we are not far off it.

From the depths of its low point at the time of the financial crisis, the S&P 500 has risen a remarkable 5.8× (and the Dow Jones Industrial Average by 4.6×). The rises in the rest of the world have been less pronounced. The MSCI World All Country Index has risen by over 300% from its trough.

Typically a pithy sobriquet is coined on each bubble; at the moment the leading contender for this fabulous bull market seems to be the 'everything bubble'. As an aside, this would be a real irony, since the intellectual underpinning for the response to the 2008 financial crisis was none other than recognition of the policy mistakes which had exacerbated the Great Depression.

For the current bull market to be extended for a meaningful timescale it is clear what is needed. To bring today's rich valuations back into line with historical experience, a period of rapid sustained economic growth in real terms is required. This in turn implies a step change in productivity growth. Whilst it is true that higher nominal growth will also reduce the debt burden, it only does so if inflation remains dormant, otherwise there would be a real danger that interest costs would rise in parallel. It is real growth that is required.

The focus therefore needs to be on what might cause a rapid lift in secular real economic growth. That means it has to be a period which achieves more than a V-shaped recovery that simply makes up the ground lost during the pandemic.

For some economies, even a V-shape may be problematic. According to the Bank of England, for example, although the UK's rate of recovery from a record 9% fall in output in 2020 is encouraging, the UK economy has still lost two years of growth as a result of the pandemic.

Let us consider the possible routes to higher real economic growth in turn:

- demographics
- trade
- migration
- productivity/technology.

Demographics

The story on demographics is relatively straightforward. Demographics are an important determinant of many aspects of an economy's progress. The age structure of the population impacts productivity, trade balances, savings and investment, and demand for financial assets. The history of demographics in modern times has been one of falling fertility rates combined with declining mortality rates as nutrition and public health improved.

On the fertility side, there has been the added influence of urbanisation, which reduced the need for large families, the increased availability of birth control and the rising costs of child-rearing and education. Set against this was the post-war baby boom and the subsequent 'echo' as the boomers had their own children.

Demographic structure is often expressed in terms of the dependency ratio. From figure 25, it can be seen that the dependency ratio was on a gently falling trend until it reached an inflection point roughly ten years ago, at which point it began to rise. On current fertility and mortality assumptions, the ratio is projected to continue to rise through to the middle of this century. Whilst minor changes in assumptions can have very significant compounding effects on future forecasts, the historic trend and future path is clear.

The post-war world economy benefitted from a growing population and declining dependency ratio, but this is now reversing. Life expectancy has increased, and with it the median age of population. In the United States, for example, life expectancy in 1900 was 50; today it is 80. With the birth rate declining and limited migration, there is nothing to prevent the ageing of populations.

Figure 25: World total dependency ratio

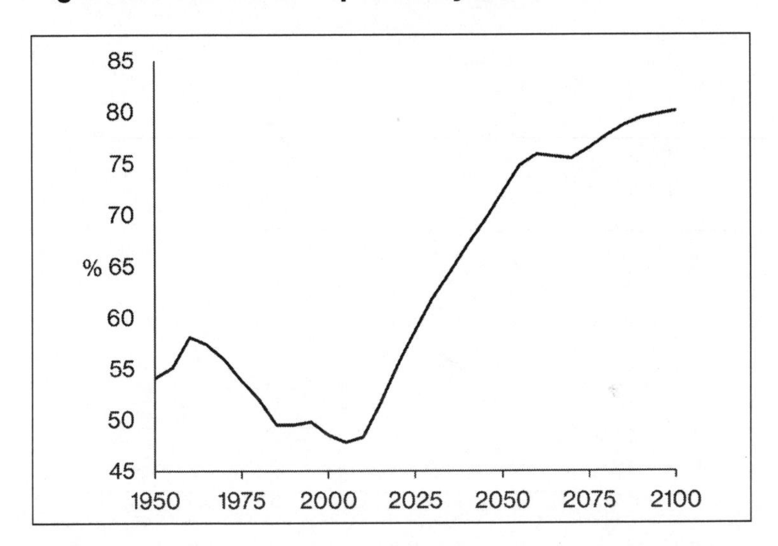

Source: United Nations, Department of Economic and Social Affairs, Population Division (2019). World Population Prospects 2019, custom data acquired via website.

Figure 26: World proportion of population aged 0–14

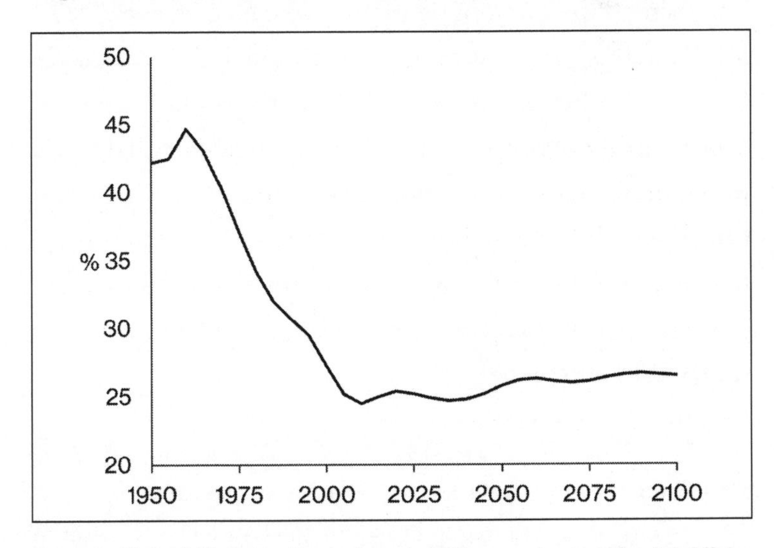

Source: United Nations, Department of Economic and Social Affairs, Population Division (2019). World Population Prospects 2019, custom data acquired via website.

Figure 27: World population 65+

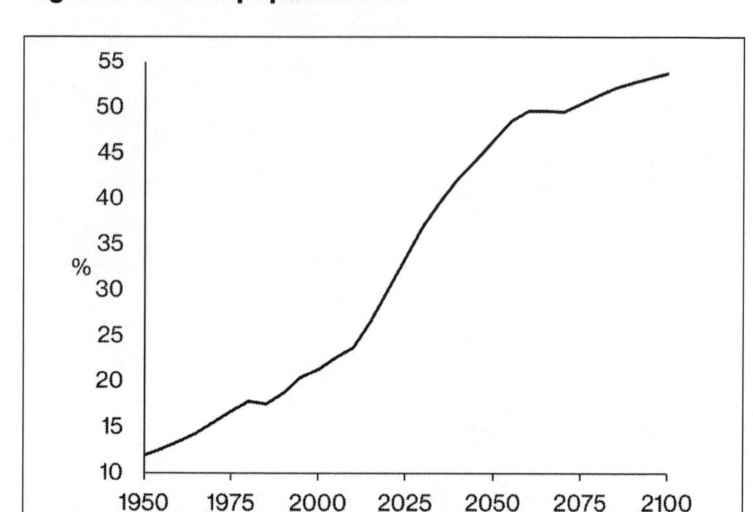

Source: United Nations, Department of Economic and Social Affairs, Population Division (2019). World Population Prospects 2019, custom data acquired via website.

The rising population-dependency ratio is consistent across most nations, with the major exception being Africa. In China the phenomenon is particularly pronounced. In other words, the proportion of actively engaged will decline, while the elderly group requiring support will increase. China is well aware of the economic and political issues that this will engender and, having relaxed the one-child policy to permit two children, is now actively promoting a three-child outcome.[30]

---

30 *The Economist*, 2021. 'A third is the word: China rapidly shifts from a two-child to a three-child policy'. Available at: www.economist.com/china/2021/06/03/china-rapidly-shifts-from-a-two-child-to-a-three-child-policy

If nothing else changes, this suggests that labour markets will be tighter and taxes will have to be higher. The academic economists Goodhart and Pradham have produced a clear and concise book which sets out the economic impact of changing demographics.[31] The critical conclusion is that the world has benefitted from a 50-year tailwind which is blowing itself out and will soon create a significant headwind for future economic growth. There is of course an inherent contradiction between policies to promote population growth and the need to reduce carbon emissions.

Figure 28: Major economies' dependency ratios

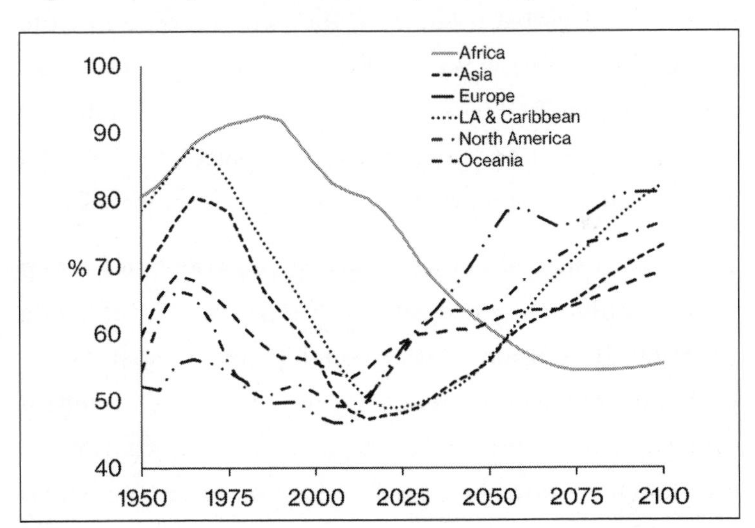

Source: United Nations, Department of Economic and Social Affairs, Population Division (2019). World Population Prospects 2019, custom data acquired via website.

31 Goodhart, C. and Pradham, M., 2020. *The Great Demographic Reversal*. London: Palgrave Macmillan.

Trade

The past 40 years have witnessed dramatic changes in the structure of the world economy. The emergence of China, and the rise of "socialism with Chinese characteristics"[32] under Deng Xiaoping, introduced a new economic powerhouse to the global economy. Similarly, although more chaotic, the fall of the Iron Curtain released the commodity riches of the former Soviet Union onto global markets, while also further freeing up global trade.

The impact of these two seismic events can be seen in the explosion of global trade from the early 1980s. Since the turn of the century, however, the growth in global trade has slowed, punctuated by a number of recessions. The days of rapid growth in trade are likely to be replaced with ones in which trade at best merely grows in line with global GDP.

There is a second, more negative, outcome, reflecting concerns about security of supplies in an era of rising geopolitical tensions. It is highly likely that many corporations will no longer wish to rely on single sourcing for their supplies. Fear of the strategic dangers of dependence on a single country or region where political action could potentially disrupt the flow of goods and components has

---

32 Xiaoping, D., 1984. 'Building a socialism with a specifically Chinese character'. *The People's Daily*, [online] Available at: www.chinadaily.com.cn/china/19thcpcnationalcongress/2010-10/21/content_29714485.htm

resonated in corporate boardrooms when risk matrices are being discussed.

The trade and security disputes between the USA and China have further highlighted the fragility of single sourcing and just-in-time supply chains, despite the greater efficiency gains and cost reductions that they made possible (thus enhancing profitability). It is inevitable that some of these gains will be lost as multiple sourcing replaces any single sourcing and inventories are required in the supply chain.

Figure 29: World total merchandise exports

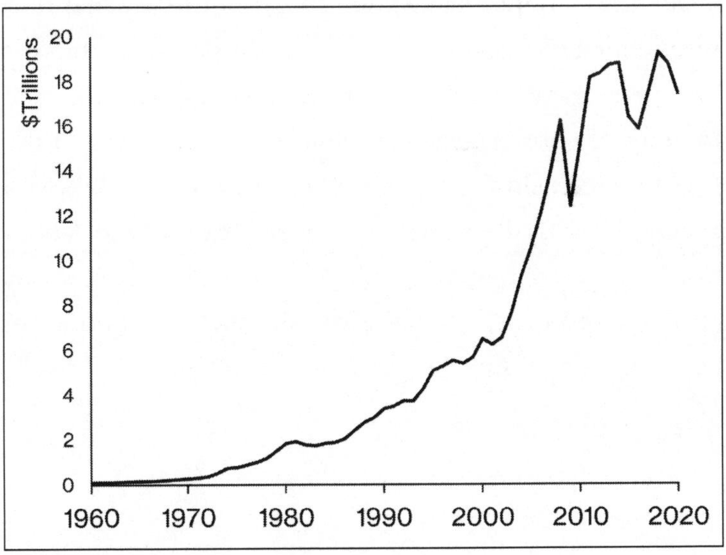

Source: Refinitiv Datastream, IMF-Direction of Trade Statistics

Migration

The topic of migration is always a sensitive one, given political and nationalistic connotations. The United States, although a country built on waves of inward migration, has recently seen growing popular anger aimed at both the level of immigration and particular migrant groups. This is not a new phenomenon, nor is it limited to the US as other examples of the time show.

Throughout the 1800s, almost all immigrant groups were vilified at one time or another. Political cartoons of the time illustrate the depth of feeling. This is not to say that they represented mainstream opinion but simply that at the very least there was a vocal constituency that could be harnessed to political ends. This was evidenced in the passing of the US Chinese Exclusion Act of 1882 and history is replete with examples across the globe. The threat of new 'cheap' labour which might threaten existing employment has always elicited a response, particularly where such a response can be focussed on a specific nationality or religion.

Figure 30: Vilification of migrants: a part of history

© 'Their New Jerusalem', Grant E. Hamilton, *Judge magazine*, 1892, from Cornell University: Persuasive Cartography: The PJ Mode Collection (Wikimedia Commons).

© Cartoon from *The Bulletin*, 1886 (Wikimedia Commons).

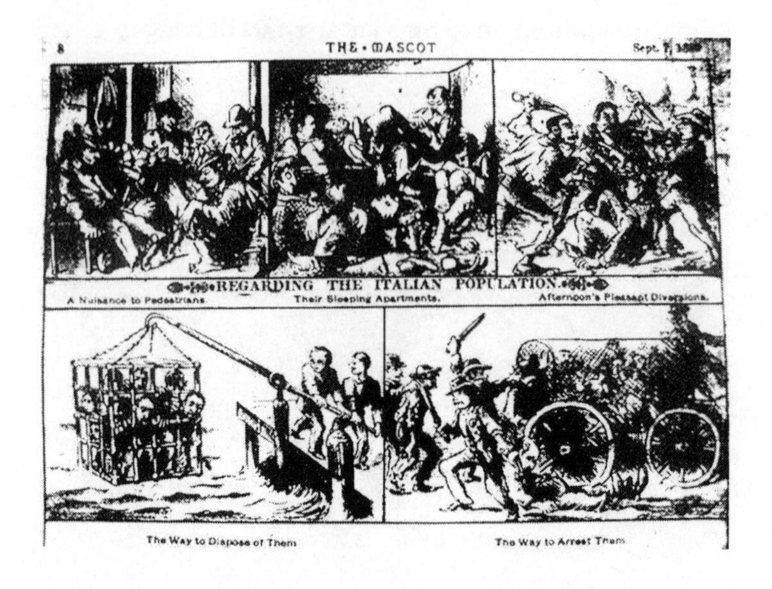

© Cartoon from *The Mascot*, New Orleans, September 7, 1889 (Wikimedia Commons)

Set against this are multiple studies that demonstrate the longer-term benefits of migration – but these benefits are not always recognised at the time. During periods of slow or negative economic growth, the perception is that jobs are being 'stolen', either by an influx of migrant labour or the offshoring of production to countries with lower wages. While this reaction is not limited to one section of society, it is most commonly found and exploited among those lacking formal education and marketable skills.

Those without a high school diploma are the most susceptible segment of society, as unemployment rates tend to be higher and more sensitive to economic activity. The rise of populist politicians in many countries since the global financial crisis is clearly related to the lack of long-term real income growth for those without specialist skill sets.

Figure 31: US unemployment by educational attainment

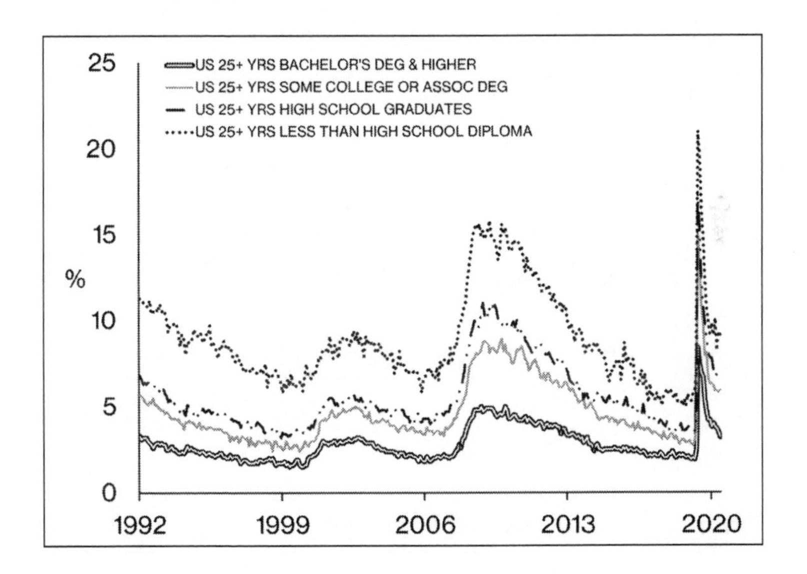

Source: Refinitiv Datastream, Bureau of Labor Statistics

In the United States, for example, the growing divergence in incomes between different segments of the working population has become more and more obvious. For the majority of the working population, real earnings have grown very slowly over the past 40 years. For top earners, the experience has been different. The income of the top 0.01% of earners has grown 15 times faster than that of the bottom 90%, whose real earnings have grown by just 25% in the past 40 years (and most of that increase was recorded before 2000). Those with the lowest incomes of all have effectively seen no growth in real incomes at all.

Figure 32: Differential US earnings growth

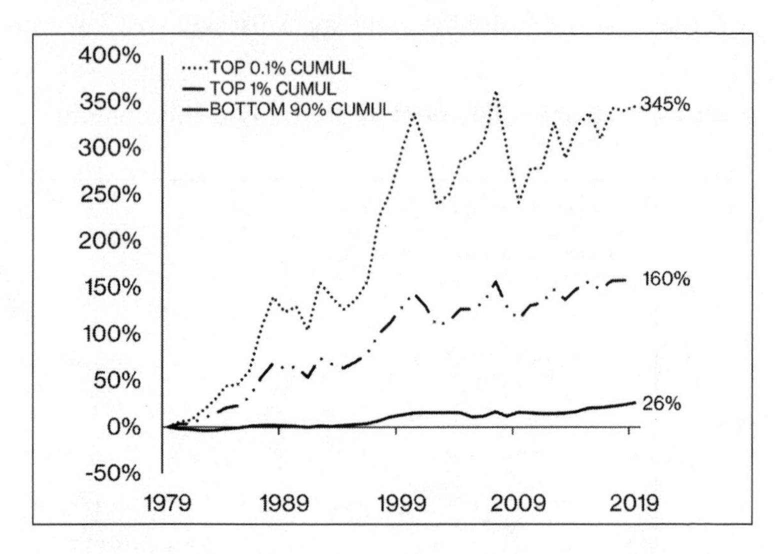

Source: Economic Policy Institute, State of Working America Data Library, 2019

Figure 33: It is all about the top end

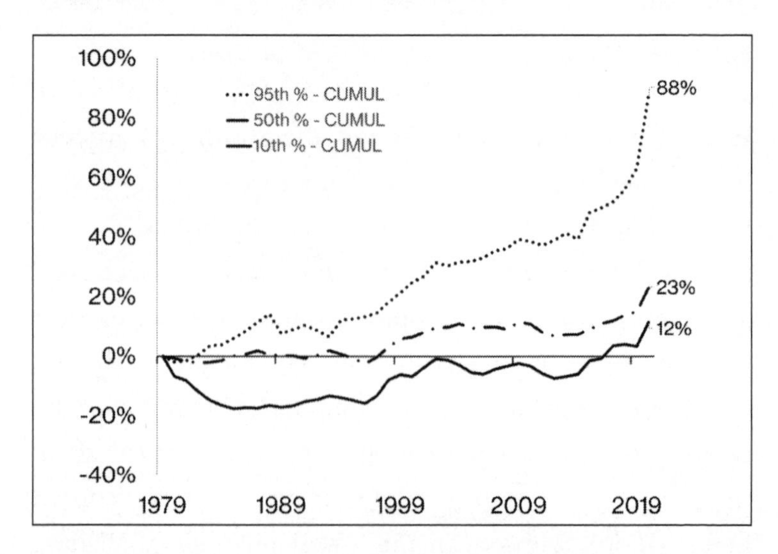

Source: Economic Policy Institute, State of Working America Data Library, 2019

While there have been other contributors to the growth of nationalist populism, exemplified by the election of Donald Trump as president, there is no doubt that stagnating wages and difficult unemployment experiences have been central to the phenomenon.

The backlash against immigration has not been limited to North America. It can be observed in the Brexit vote in the United Kingdom and in the rise of right-wing nationalist parties across Europe. It is likely therefore to take some time before the pushback against immigration, and its role in the slowing of economic growth, can be reversed. As long as it persists, it will contribute to the tightening of labour markets and inflationary pressures, as well as to supply restrictions on some goods and services.

Productivity

The evidence all points to the fact that trade, demographics and migration are no longer going to be supporting economic growth in the way that they have been since the opening of the world economy in the 1990s. In reality, what were a series of tailwinds may well be turning into a headwind.

That leaves improving productivity as the remaining hope for the world to achieve the required sustainable real growth in economic activity over the next 20–30 years. Explaining what is happening to productivity unfortunately remains a big puzzle for the economics profession. Defining and measuring productivity is fraught with technical difficulties.

How, for example, does one measure productivity gains when product quality and capability are improving so rapidly all the time? One only needs to think about the range of products from mobile phones to semiconductors and automobiles to understand how difficult it is to calculate productivity improvements against rapidly changing product specifications.

Similarly, there can be lags between the introduction of a new technology and its eventual impact on productivity. This is the so-called Solow Paradox, named after the American economist Robert Solow, who quipped in 1987 that: "You can see the computer age everywhere but in the productivity statistics."[33]

By the mid-1990s, according to one recent study, "many economic observers acknowledge the extraordinary contributions of information technology (IT) to U.S. economic growth".[34] Yet these productivity gains from technological advances were slow to show up in short-term aggregate data for economic growth.

It seems logical that there will in due course be an increase in productivity flowing from the many technological

---

33 Solow, R., 1987. Book Review. *New York Times*, p.36.

34 Brill, M., Chansky, B. and Kim, J., 2018. 'Multifactor productivity slowdown in U.S. manufacturing'. *Monthly Labor Review, U.S. Bureau of Labor Statistics*, July.

advances of the past decade. In the healthcare industry, for example, productivity started to tail off after 2000, under the influence of expiring patents and greater competition from cheaper generic drugs.

More recently, however, stunning advances in the scientific understanding of the genome make it likely that many more drugs can be produced to treat specific conditions effectively, and at much greater speed than in the past. The fact that pharmaceutical companies were able to produce effective vaccines against Covid-19 in a matter of weeks is a good example of how well this might play out.

Some of the greatest gains from information technology have been created in the arena of price discovery. For example, it is much harder now for companies to charge premium prices, given how easy the internet and price-comparison sites make it for consumers to shop around and compare competing offers. That contributes directly to an increase in consumer welfare, enabling them to buy more for less.

Despite these examples of positive developments, it remains the case that productivity has shown little sign of accelerating. To the contrary, if anything productivity has been falling in some sectors, at least as recorded in official economic statistics. How can that be explained? Some attribute the decline to insufficient investment and the perverse effect of current senior management incentives, which favour buying back shares over investing in new growth opportunities.

Others suggest that, as impressive as recent technological advances may be, they are no greater than those which were seen at the end of the 19th century and in the early 20th century (e.g., planes, trains and automobiles, the telephone).[35] The debate goes on.

The main point is that there is little evidence at the moment to suggest that we are on the verge of a new growth miracle driven by improved productivity. Table 3 provides a simple illustration with a crude measure of average US productivity (output per head) in the decades from the 1950s onwards relative to GDP. Despite all the advances over the period, productivity growth largely resided in the 2–2.5% range. Arguably the most recent decade can be seen as an anomaly where the impact of the GFC offset some of the internet-related gains. The point is that whilst we can expect a Covid-related rebound, financial salvation is unlikely to come from this source.

---

35 Gordon, R., 2016. *The Rise and Fall of American Growth.* Princeton and Oxford: Princeton University Press.

Table 3: US Labour Productivity and Economic Growth

	Growth Output/Head*	Growth Real GDP
1950s	3.0	4.1
1960s	2.1	4.2
1970s	1.7	3.3
1980s	1.7	3.2
1990s	2.5	3.3
2000s	2.5	1.8
2010s	0.4	2.1

*Labour productivity, non-financial corporations, output per hour
Source: Bureau of Labor Statistics, U.S. Department of Labor

What the evidence *does* suggest is that whatever productivity growth there has been, little of the benefit has accrued to traditional labour (figure 35). The great majority of the rewards have instead gone to the owners of capital (or, through offshoring, potentially to workers in emerging markets). That only intensifies the contrast between the fortunes of the majority of workers in developed countries and the more privileged segments of society. This in turn further contributes to the sense of unfairness and, as a consequence, to the sense of a need for interventionist policies to address the issue.

Figure 34: Productivity growth falling

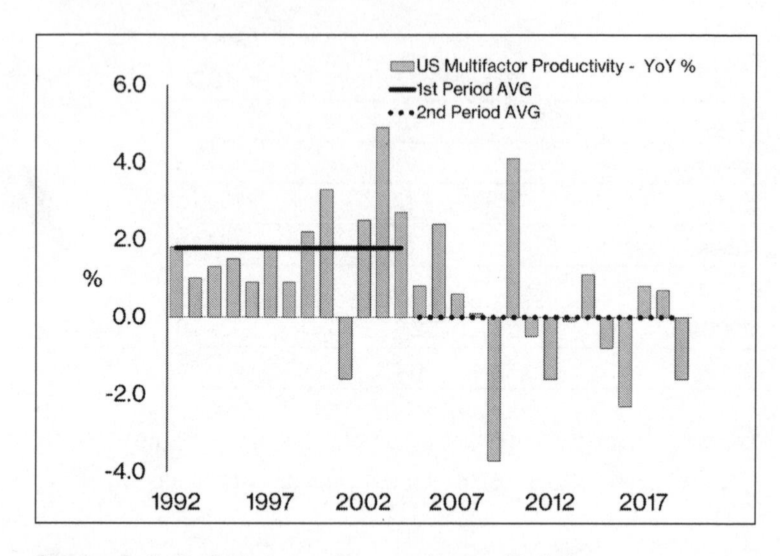

Source: Refinitiv Datastream, Bureau of Labor Statistics

Figure 35: Productivity growth benefits not flowing to labour

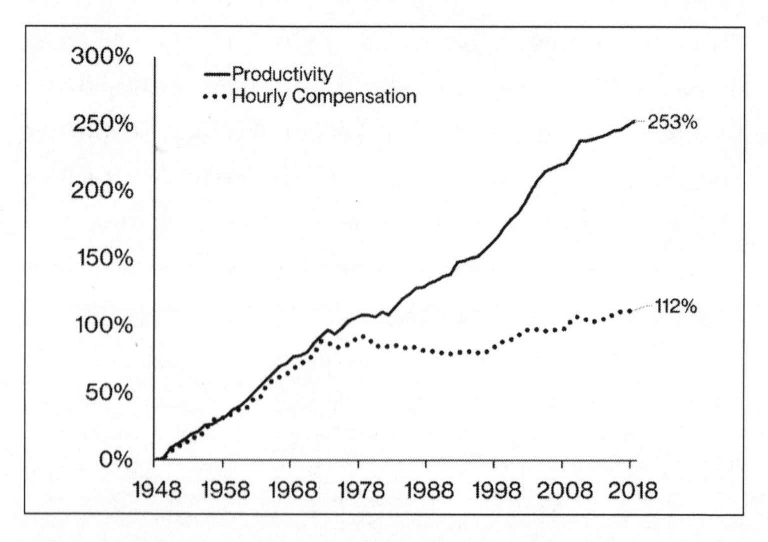

Source: Economic Policy Institute, State of Working America Data Library, 2019

A final comment on economic growth flows from the pressing need to deal with global warming. Since the start of the industrial revolution, the world has struggled (and largely failed) to deal with the negative externalities associated with the polluting consequences of economic progress. Apart from action to deal with catastrophic events such as oil spills, polluters have largely been able to avoid accounting for the cost of their actions on the environment.

Whether you take agriculture, industrial production or transport, growth has mostly been allowed to take precedence over the negative side effects. The scientific evidence behind the coming threat from climate change is overwhelming, and whilst the world will react slowly with remedial measures, it seems clear that the necessary measures will be taken in due course. The move towards electric vehicles and carbon trading is just an early example of what will unfold.

As an aside, many investment opportunities will emerge as a result of the drive to mitigate the effects of climate change. This is a potentially combustible mix. Investors will continue to face pressure to support companies that are carbon neutral, or in the business of carbon reduction. As the carbon-reduction industry is in its infancy, there is currently a shortage of potential investments relative to the supply of capital.

History shows[36] that supply always responds to such a demand overhang, while investors often suspend critical judgment in favour of a 'blue sky' conceptual approach, particularly when the cost of capital is low, as it is today. This pattern has already begun, and while legitimate and profitable winners will emerge in this area, there will also be many losers and more than a few less-scrupulous operators launching companies to take advantage of investors' less-discerning approach.

However, notwithstanding the critical importance of pollution reduction, internalising the negative external costs will do little to enhance GDP growth. Alternative forms of energy and the supporting infrastructure may well see their costs fall below those of hydrocarbon-based incumbents, but this will take time and capital. For an extended period, the shorter-term impact is likely to dampen productivity growth and profitability. Without offsetting fiscal injections, GDP growth is likely therefore to be lower than in a world without carbon-neutral initiatives.

---

36 Nairn, A., 2018. *Engines That Move Markets: Technology Investing from Railroads to the Internet and Beyond.* 2nd ed. Petersfield: Harriman House.

The future for growth

If demographics, trade and migration are not incrementally supportive, and productivity is muted in its impact, it is hard to see how higher real economic growth can come to the rescue and resolve the twin problems of high asset valuations and the associated overhang of debt which we described earlier. Yes, there can be real growth of some kind, but will it be sufficient to resolve the imbalances which have led to the current world in which financial excesses are so evident? It is very hard to see how that can be achieved.

For historical context, figure 36 shows the recorded post-war rates of real US GDP growth. At the risk of grossly oversimplifying, before 2000 the trend rate of growth was somewhere around 3.5%, although already on a declining trend. Since 2000, the rate of real growth has been much lower, averaging somewhere around 2%. This would also be consistent with the secular changes in demographics and other factors mentioned above.

Figure 36: Real US GDP growth declining

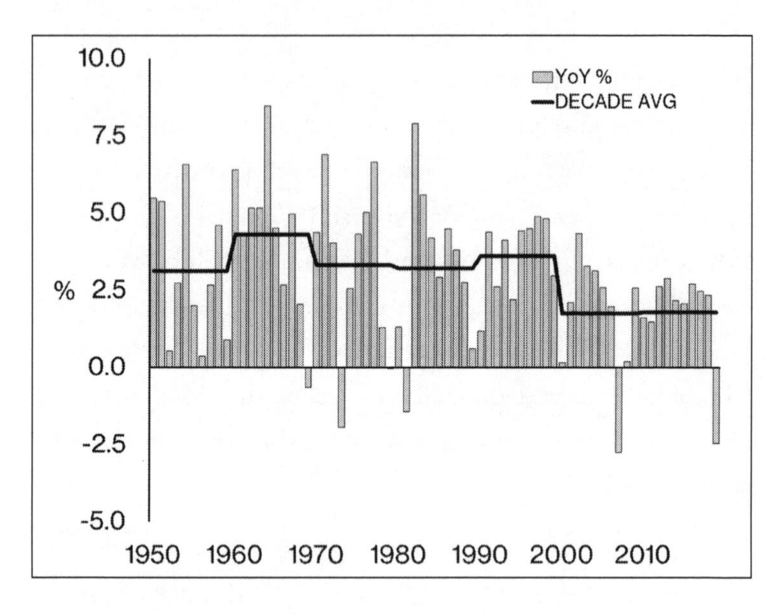

Source: Global Financial Data

If one is going to speculate about future growth and real interest rates, the above historic experience is helpful in setting some guiderails. An optimistic outlook would suggest 3% is possible, but this does require something to counteract the negative trends already noted. A 4% growth rate would represent a modern historic high, requiring productivity advances similar to the peak post-war years. Recent trends would suggest a secular number more in line with 2%. In the very short run, the picture remains clouded by the Covid economic recovery. One by-product of the various government support schemes has been hoarding of cash by households above historical levels. As this unwinds it has created a mini-consumption boom which assists economic growth. While this will necessarily be of limited duration, it could have the effect of sustaining asset market confidence as long as it persists.

The other side of the coin is that the cash bonanza has effectively been funded by government at the cost of an ever larger fiscal deficit. Another argument frequently deployed in support of future asset price growth is that household confidence is high, supported by wealth increases related to both high asset prices and low debt finance costs. The argument runs that, since consumption is the largest component of developed economies, this supports confidence and household expenditure, and thus mitigates against possible recession. The circularity of this argument is obvious.

6.

Future Market Scenarios

Lessons from history

LOOKING AT HISTORIC movements in the S&P is instructive. Figure 37 details the performance of the S&P 500 index, but also includes what the index levels would have been if it were held to constant PE valuation assumptions. For simplicity, the two assumptions used are the average valuation over the post-war period and the average valuation over the period from 1870 onwards.

What is interesting is that, up to 1980 (and for most of the post-war period), the rise in the index was driven by profits growth rather than expanding valuation. Valuations did wax and wane in line with changes in investor sentiment, but over time they invariably reverted to their historic averages. The TMT bubble was a notable recent anomaly, when euphoric price rises left earnings way behind, creating stratospheric valuations in the process.

Much of the discussion around the disruptive effect of the internet was accurate, but as share prices rose investors became ever more indiscriminate on the potential beneficiaries and ever less sceptical on the revenue and valuation case. Anything that could be remotely linked to the internet would be awarded a premium valuation. Eventually, reality dawned and prices returned to earth in the 2000–03 bear market. Just as an aside, I can clearly remember an investment case being made for a furniture manufacturer based on the premise that it supported the development of the internet because it made the tables on which PCs could be placed!

The fall in share prices revealed both many flawed business cases and multiple instances of outright fraud. However, it also provided an environment where investors were then able to survey the wreckage and begin to pick out the long-term winners in the internet space. It was not during the euphoric bubble-inflating years that investors reaped rewards. The gains made during that period largely evaporated in the market collapse.

The sustainable gains accrued to investors who had sufficient liquidity to build positions in the period *after* the bubble had burst. The parallel today is that the deviation between earnings growth and valuations we have seen develop since the GFC is of a similar order of magnitude to that which produced the TMT bubble. The S&P 500 is trading on more than twice the long-term average PE ratio.

This is another way of observing that the stock market is being priced for perfection. It is not that technology has failed to produce some long-term winners, nor that more will not emerge. As Figure 37 shows however, the clear message to emerge from today's valuations is that the S&P could drop by 50% and still only return to its long-term average valuation.

Figure 37: S&P by PE

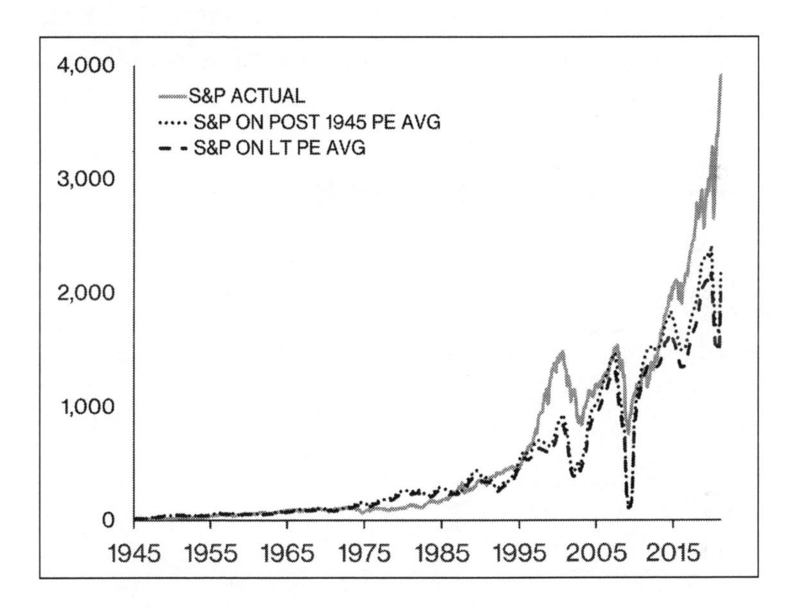

Sources: Robert J. Shiller, www.econ.yale.edu; Edinburgh Partners

As noted earlier, there is a reasonable counter argument that valuations based on single-year earnings are not very meaningful during cyclical lows, let alone a period when we have experienced a pandemic and an unprecedented economic shutdown. The Shiller PE, or CAPE, is again more helpful in this regard, given its use of ten-year average earnings. It, too, however shows a very similar picture: of a bull market that has been driven by expanding valuations, rather than by increases in earnings.

The bottom line is this: to return to its post-war average, the S&P would need to fall by 45%. This, not uncoincidentally, is almost exactly the fall that occurred when the TMT bubble eventually burst. It is not encouraging to note that, in the past, when inflation has been sustained above 4%, the CAPE PE has tended to trade at a discount to its long-term average – so there is a real danger of an overshoot if inflation does become an issue again.

Figure 38: S&P by CAPE (Shiller) PE

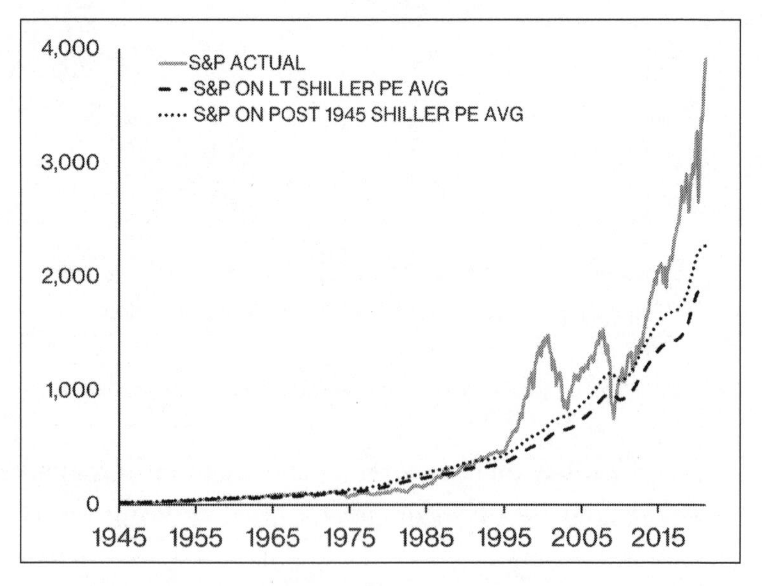

Sources: Robert J. Shiller, www.econ.yale.edu; Edinburgh Partners

The CAPE PE is also shown in log form in figure 39 to allow a more accurate historical comparison. Log charts capture the rate of change in prices, not just the absolute movement up and down of index numbers. The chart highlights the extended periods in which valuations have inflated returns. It also highlights the inflationary period of the 1970s, when equities reacted to economic conditions by trading at a discount to historic valuations.

Figure 39: S&P by CAPE (Shiller) PE: log scale

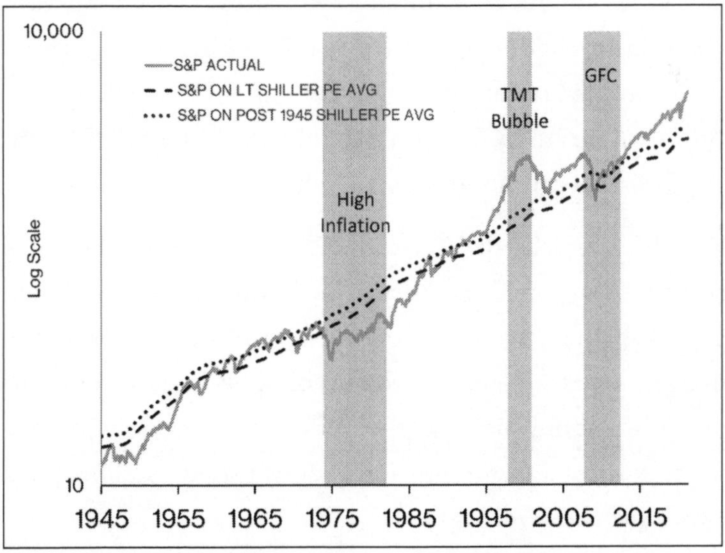

Sources: Robert J. Shiller, www.econ.yale.edu; Edinburgh Partners

While it would take a near halving of the S&P to return to a historic average CAPE valuation (assuming no change in earnings), there is of course an alternative scenario in which we *do* see rapid earnings growth. This would also help to bring the PE and CAPE back down to nearer the long-term average. How much growth would be required?

This is a relatively straight forward question to answer, but it does require making some broad assumptions about future economic growth.

Given the relationship between GDP growth and earnings, and realistic forecasts for future GDP and inflation, it is a simple arithmetic task to plot what might happen to the cyclically adjusted PE, or CAPE, of the US stock market under a range of different scenarios. The long-term relationship between US GDP and EPS is reasonably stable, with corporate earnings growing at somewhere between 1.5× and 2× the rate of GDP growth, although the relationship tends not to capture the deep cyclical movements that well.

For the scenario analysis, the EPS used for 2021 and 2022 assumes continued recovery from Covid. The 2021 estimate is 21% higher than the 2019 pre-Covid out-turn and the 2022 figure is 7.5% higher than 2021. This is consistent with the more optimistic end of sell-side forecasts as of May 2021. The one-year assumption for 2023 is varied to allow for a more sustained recovery.

Thereafter, a 'long-term' average GDP growth rate is used. This assumption is varied at 2%, 3% and 4%, which ranges from slightly above that recorded in the past 20 years to slightly above the highest average achieved since 1950. The underlying assumptions are based on those provided by the Federal Reserve, the Congressional Budget Office and a range of private sector 'sell-side' forecasts.

To give a historic context to the earnings assumptions, a log chart of the three earnings assumptions is shown in figure 40. This can serve as a reality check to the assumptions being used. The chart shows persistent and significant earnings growth, at a rate of change which is higher than the long-term average. You cannot reasonably say that these assumptions are unduly pessimistic!

Figure 40: Log scale real EPS with 2%, 3%, 4% GDP growth assumption from 2023 onwards

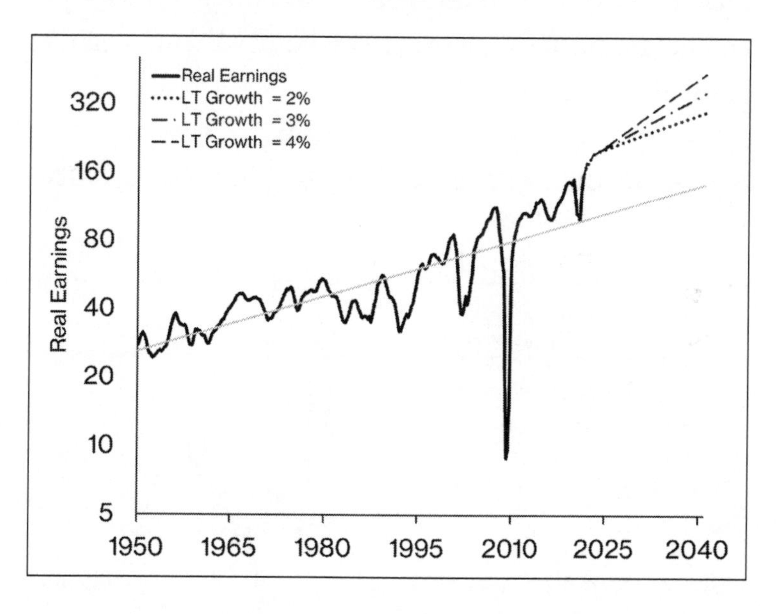

Sources: Robert J. Shiller, www.econ.yale.edu; Edinburgh Partners

Let's look at the results if we take a 3% real growth rate in 2023 and long-term assumptions of 2%, 3% and 4% per annum thereafter. What stands out is that it would take at least five years for the US CAPE to cease being more than one standard deviation above the average and ten years, even on the most optimistic assumptions, for the US CAPE to return to its long-term average purely as a result of earnings growth.

Not surprisingly, the outcome is sensitive to the near-term earnings assumptions, which are more likely to prove optimistic than pessimistic. The obvious conclusion is that while there could be sufficient time for corporate earnings to grow and bring valuations back to their historic average, they will only do so if investors make no real return from equities for the next ten years! This is not what most market participants are currently assuming.

Figure 41: US CAPE under 2%, 3% and 4% real GDP growth assumptions

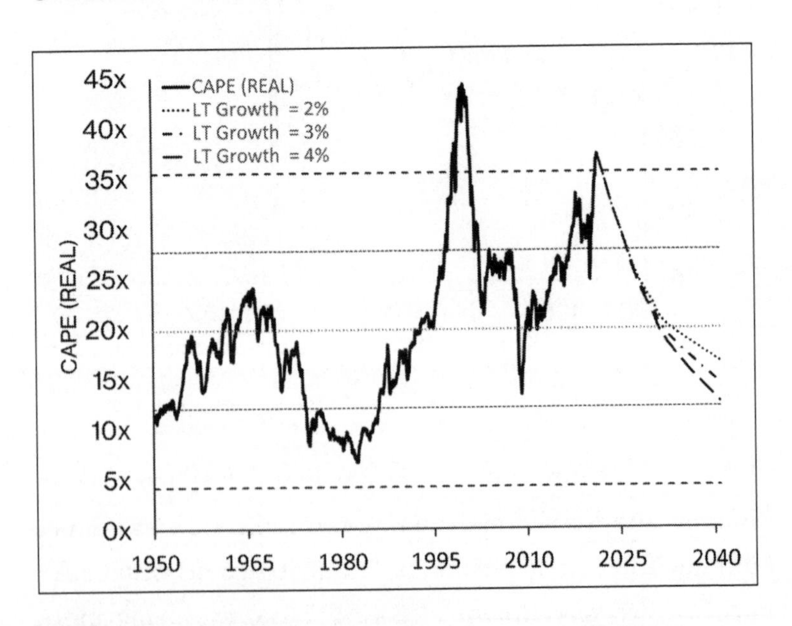

Sources: Robert J. Shiller, www.econ.yale.edu; Edinburgh Partners

The CAPE chart shows the profile of the cyclically adjusted PE with the EPS derived from the three different long-term real GDP growth assumptions. Whilst 2% real GDP growth, and perhaps even at a stretch 3%, might not seem unreasonable from a historical perspective, 4% would be a historical outlier if it were to happen, even before taking into account the structural headwinds to growth identified earlier.

However, even if 4% is deemed reasonable, it still presents a hurdle for investors. Is it also reasonable to reach a conclusion that investors will be happy to wait ten years in order to achieve a real return? The only explanation that could justify such optimism is that we are in a new era where such valuations can be sustained and even expand, or to use a previous quote can be thought to have reached "what looks like a permanently high plateau".

If we approach the analysis from a different perspective, we can ask: instead of questioning what would it take for the S&P index to be validated by higher corporate earnings, what would be required for the S&P to fall to less than one standard deviation above its historic average within ten years? The answer is clear: it would involve a prolonged bear market on a scale to match those that were observed from 2000 to 2003 and from 2007 to 2009.

This is just another way of saying that current valuations, on any rational analysis, are not consistent with a world in which growth is constrained and government debt levels are at extreme highs. Barring some kind of economic growth miracle, this suggests that a stock market correction on a historic scale is inevitable. Only the existence of the central bank 'put', the idea that any sign of market panic will produce a soothing policy response, appears to be keeping markets at these historically high levels.

This puts the central banks in an extremely delicate position. If the economy is robust, what is the justification for continued intervention? If the economy overheats and inflation becomes entrenched, how can they continue to justify such loose monetary policy and yet still retain the confidence of the markets?

If, on the other hand, the economy weakens and debt defaults start to emerge, how can any fresh intervention avoid the trap of moral hazard, rewarding imprudent borrowers and poor lending practices, precipitating another debt crisis like the one that triggered the 2008 crash?

Yet there is little sign to date that policymakers are thinking about withdrawing the 'put' any time soon. Although Covid decimated the global economy in 2020, resulting in a massive increase in government debt and a sharp fall in both bond yields and the stock market, all it took for markets to recover was reassurance that policymakers still had their backs. Bond yields have pulled back and the US stock market not only recovered all its lost ground by the end of the year, but went on to hit new all-time highs.

The question to ask at the end of this analysis is simple: how long can this fragile valuation edifice survive? In some ways the 'put' is an illusion, the equivalent of a three-card trick. The taper tantrum in 2013, when Ben Bernanke suggested a gradual withdrawal of QE, shows how vulnerable the edifice is. Given how rapidly central bank balance sheets have expanded since then, it is hard to believe that markets will react any less negatively to any future change in central bank policy.

7.

The Past as a Guide to the Future

MEAN-REVERSION ACTS AS an anchor in investment. At the individual company level, it can be highly misleading. For example, knowing that a company has earned a particular profit margin in the past is only meaningful if the future is the same as the past, a dubious assumption in a world of innovation and economic Darwinism, where the average life of a publicly listed company is only around two decades.

At an aggregate market level, the conclusion is far more reliable, as the individual winners and losers largely cancel out. History suggests that the long-term real return in equities is determined by a range of factors which change only slowly. The foregoing analysis implies that many of the structural factors which have provided positive support for economic growth have now passed an inflection point.

It is logical to use a historic valuation framework to provide an idea of the path that asset prices may take. Unless productivity can come to the rescue, which is possible but unlikely, economic growth is unlikely to return to the levels seen in the second half of the 20th century. In those circumstances, it would clearly be bold to assume that the long-term real return from equities can remain unchanged. It certainly won't be going up.

The annual Equity Gilt Study[37] produced by Barclays is an outstanding repository of returns information. The data runs from the mid-1920s and it is therefore possible to get a long-term perspective on returns. The last time the US had debt levels comparable to today was at the end of World War II. The experience for debtholders over the period to the mid-1980s, when it then troughed, is instructive.

Figure 42 shows the cumulative real return from holding US bonds from 1945, the last time debt to GDP was at equivalent levels to today (see figure 44). One can clearly see how poor an investment bonds were over that period, with purchasing power sustaining significant losses right through to the 1970s. The final inflationary burst was only ended with the arrival of the Volcker Federal Reserve. The inflationary experience is detailed in figure 45.

---

37 2021. *Equity Gilt Study*. London: Barclays.

Figure 42: Real US bond cumulative return (1945=100)

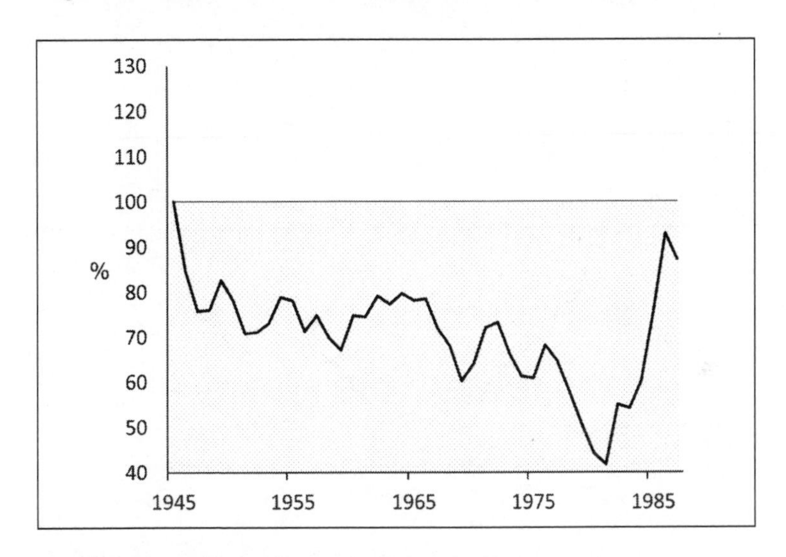

Source: Barclays Bond Equity Gilt Study 2020

Figure 43: US 10-year nominal yield

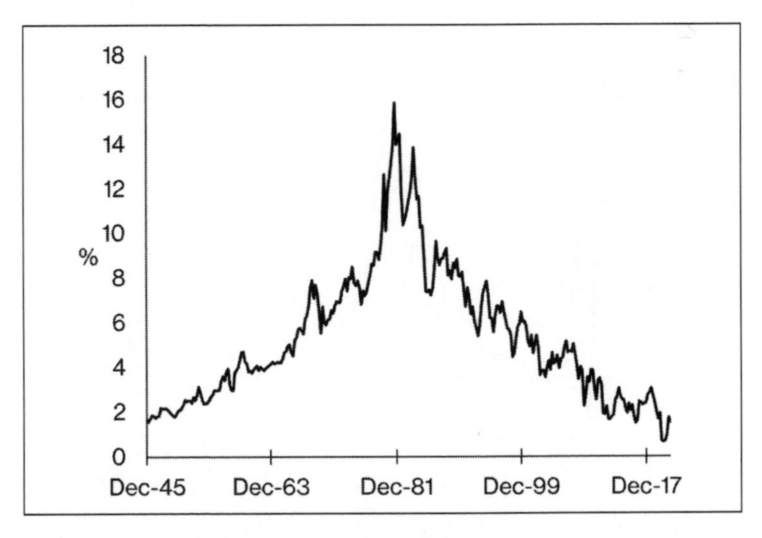

Source: Refinitiv Datastream; Economic Report of the President, Econ. Rept. 2013 – Table B-73: Bond yields and interest rates, 1941–2012

Figure 44: US debt/GDP

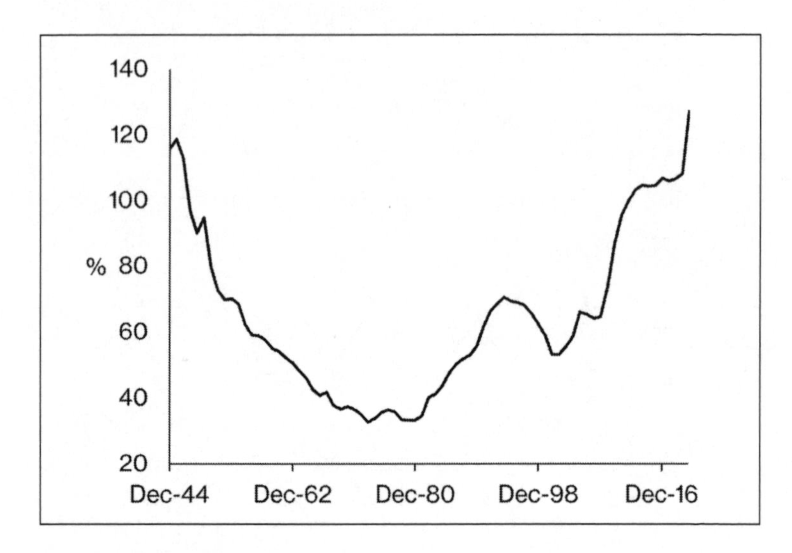

Source: Global Financial Data

Figure 45: US CPI

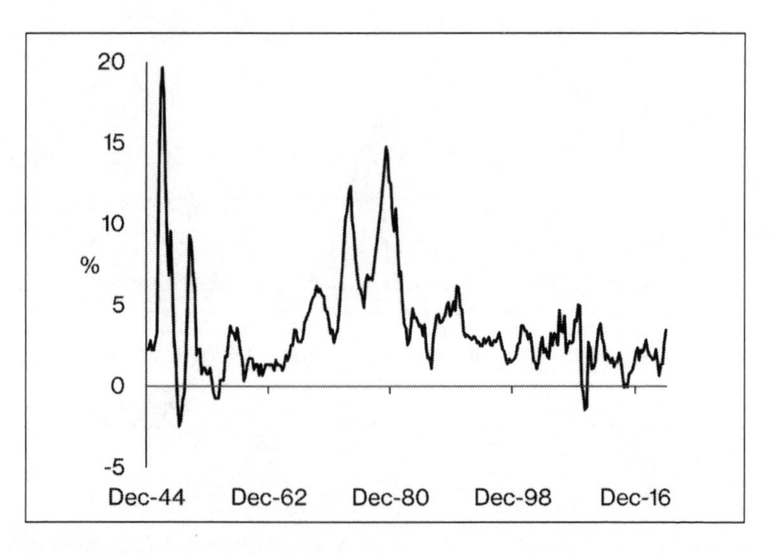

Source: Global Financial Data

To summarise:

- In 1945 inflation was 2.3% (end 2020, 1.3%) and the ten-year bond yield 2.36% (end 2020, 0.89%)
- In 1945 the ratio of debt/GDP is broadly equivalent to today's levels, which look likely to continue to rise.
- From 1945, a US bondholder only made a positive real return if they held those bonds until 1986, four decades later.
- Holding US bonds for the 35 years from 1945 to 1980 would have created losses of 60% in real terms.
- The return to positive returns was the result of the Federal Reserve's assault on inflation under Paul Volcker.

All in all, over the course of three decades, bonds failed to act as a safe haven, instead recording dismal returns. This resulted largely because the starting nominal yield was low and for several years lagged inflation, which, outside of the immediate post-war spike, itself picked up slowly at first, before accelerating from the late 1960s onwards, culminating in a brutal bear market in the 1970s

Bonds: how the frog was boiled

The frog-boiling myth suggests that if a frog is dropped into boiling water it will jump out immediately, but if the temperature rises from cold to boiling point gradually, it will suffer paralysis and die before it realises what is happening and can jump out. Leaving aside the biological inaccuracy, it does provide a good analogy for the post-war bond experience.

The key to deflating away a government debt overhang is ensuring that inflation, or the fear of inflation, does not cause the cost of debt servicing to rise and offset the inflationary impact. This inflationary impact is effectively bond holders paying for past government expenditure by inflation-induced loss of purchasing power. There are a number of tools that governments can deploy to support this outcome. Collectively they have become known as 'financial repression'.[38]

When successful, the impact of financial repression on effective debt reduction can be extremely powerful. For example, it has been estimated that inflation between 1946 and 1955 reduced US debt/GDP by approximately 40%.[39] If

---

38 McKinnon, R., 1973. *Money and Capital in Economic Development.* Washington, D.C.: Brookings Institution.

39 Aizenman, J. and Marion, N., 2009. Using inflation to erode the U.S. public debt. *National Bureau of Economic Research: NBER Working Paper Series.*

the alternative is debt default, then repression seems almost benign by comparison. It has the added advantage, because it unfolds by stealth, of being the least politically damaging.

How, then, does financial repression work? The mechanics involve suppressing the cost of debt and allowing inflation to gradually erode the value of the principal. The tools to achieve this are relatively obvious. Firstly, a government can simply dictate the rate of interest, at least so long as there is a sufficiently large pool of domestic capital.

Secondly, a government can directly intervene to set bond prices and hence interest rates. Thirdly, a government can regulate to increase the pool of domestic capital by forcing financial institutions and pension funds to hold more government debt than they otherwise would. This is normally introduced under the banner of 'prudential regulation', and justified as protecting the financial system, although it obviously does so by harming savers or the financial institutions involved.

Fourthly, alternative asset classes can be made less attractive through the imposition of taxes (such as transaction taxes), or simply prohibitions on ownership. These would not be new policies and their historic antecedents are well documented.[40] Moreover, many of them have already been deployed as 'temporary' responses to the global financial crisis, although use of the word temporary is already

---

40 Reinhart, C. and Sbrancia, M., 2011. The Liquidation of Government Debt. *National Bureau of Economic Research: NBER Working Paper Series.*

stretching the definition of the term beyond the point the English language can bear.

Equities: the cult of the equity is born

For equity holders, the returns experience was completely different. The 35-year post-war period from 1945 to 1980 saw US equities record an annualised real return of 7%. It was during this period that the 'cult of the equity' was created, in recognition of the superior returns available to equity investors. For the first time, measuring the equity/bond yield gap became de rigeur for analysts.

Why would not the same thing happen today, when real yields are again negative? Greater equity exposure from the 1950s onwards was underpinned by growth in corporate profits and earnings, and projecting higher earnings is not an unreasonable assumption today. There are, however, two huge differences between then and now. One is that the profitability of listed companies is already at a historically high level, so there is a limit to the room for improvement in the future.

The second is that equity valuations today are so much higher than they were in the earlier period. Whereas equities were at the lower end of their historical valuation range immediately after World War II, today they are at the other end and indeed have rarely been higher. At the same time, it is also worth pointing out that equity and bond yields are now almost coincident.

The burden of argument for anyone attempting to justify current market valuations therefore lies on those seeking to do so by reference to a view that stock market valuation has moved permanently higher, just as Irving Fisher, the highly esteemed but unfortunate economist, was espousing in 1929. Given the differences between the post-war period and now, alluding to deliberately suppressed interest rates as being the new normal as a comparator stretches credulity.

A Rocky Road Ahead

NONE OF THE foregoing fills one with enthusiasm for investing in either bonds or equities. Bonds, one might say, offer nothing but return-free risk and publicly listed equities are so richly valued as to make strong future returns dependent on implausible assumptions. Privately owned equity and debt may appear less at risk, but that is almost certainly an illusion, based on the relative lack of transparency. A term that has been gaining traction is the 'everything bubble'. This appears an entirely reasonable description.

It seems safe to conclude that asset valuations are being kept aloft, to a significant extent, by the policies employed to avoid a rerun of the Great Depression after the global financial crisis. The recent pandemic has intensified the build-up of debt and to some extent may have blinded investors to the underlying issues that were already becoming apparent before the virus struck.

As discussed earlier, the apparent lack of economic consequences has helped the political orthodoxy swing firmly behind debt-financed intervention, with only political hue determining the mix of policy tools and form of intervention. Given this, it is reasonable to expect that intervention will remain important until such a time as the markets and/or public acceptance change.

It would be foolish to project just one scenario for how asset markets are likely to evolve in the coming months and years. Looking beyond the very short term, asset markets have an unpleasant asymmetric look about them. It is reasonable to project that, at best, they are set to go sideways, and at worst fall very sharply. A lot will depend on how policymakers react to what unfolds.

The reality is that every plausible scenario involves significant disappointment, not just for stock market investors but owners of other asset classes too. To use the analogy of the well-known fairy tale, given the general elevation of asset market valuations, there simply is no plausible Goldilocks scenario out there. How bad could it be?

The global bond market is $130trn in size and global equities are a $110trn market. In a nightmare scenario, both could lose value at the same time. If that were to happen, it would be echoed also in the private equity/debt and property markets which are more highly leveraged and liquidity sensitive, and so could well see prices fall even further.

A 30% decline in the value of bonds and a 30–50% decline in equities, although unlikely to be perfectly coincident, would potentially put $75-95trn of the world's apparent wealth at risk. Resetting prices to more sustainable levels will inevitably feed through as losses in almost every corner of society.

It is worth pausing to consider in context the magnitude of what is being suggested. An aggregate global decline in asset values of $70 trillion would not be far short of total global GDP and nearly 3.5x the size of the US economy. One does *not* need to suppose that all households have based their expenditure decisions on current valuations to realise that there will be a huge wealth effect should such a decline occur.

The asset price decline will create both direct negative effects and collateral damage. The general economic environment will not be an appetising one, combining business failure and rising unemployment and, potentially, continuing inflation. This will inevitably present very difficult questions for policymakers since any action is likely to exacerbate one issue as it seeks to address another.

Taking a negative view of asset markets does not mean that markets will have to fall sharply tomorrow, but it does imply that before too long they have to rebase to more realistic valuations. That could happen in one severe downward move, or it could come in phases over a more extended period.

Reverting to the analogy used earlier, as valuations move further and further away from the long-term trend, the elastic is getting more and more stretched. In the immediate future, it could stretch further. In a free market, prices are set by what the participants happen to believe is value, and there is no law that says they cannot sustain an illusion for some time.

I happen to believe we are very close to breaking point, and I am struck by the similarities between the excesses we are seeing now with the market situation in 2007[41] and 1999/2000,[42] when we saw equity overvaluation combined with lax monetary policy and unduly rosy economic expectations. This prompted me to warn of the risks of a significant stock market correction, which duly came to pass soon afterwards.

The conclusion on bonds is even more emphatic. Sovereign bond yields are often used as the 'risk-free' discount rate in the analysis which underpins asset prices. This is not unreasonable given their government backing, but the reasonableness remains only so long as their prices are determined by markets rather than by governments. Where governments are key, describing sovereign bonds as offering return-free risk rather than the traditional description of risk-free return is sadly justified.[43]

Calling market tops is of course a dangerous occupation, particularly when central banks are invested so heavily in trying to keep valuations aloft. There is an old market saying that "they do not ring a bell at the top of the market". This

---

41 Nairn, A., 2007. 'Time to Hunker Down'. *Independent Investor.*

42 'This time is different' March 2000, Franklin Templeton

43 Grant, J., 2008. 'Insight: Return-free risk'. *Financial Times.*

may be true, but there are so many signs of excess in market valuations today that even the most hardened optimists are surely experiencing some form of tinnitus.

What might act as a trigger to cause the eventual shattering of the framework which allows current market valuations to persist? Looking back at past periods of financial excess, any number of things could trigger a market reaction. Sometimes it has been something that appeared at first sight to be inconsequential.

For example, the Bundesbank nudging rates higher from a low base in 1987 did not itself cause a cataclysmic economic event. It simply signalled that there might be a reversal in policy – but that proved to be enough to prompt the markets to rethink all their assumptions. The merger of AOL and Time Warner in 2000 was a sensible decision by AOL to utilise its overvalued equity to buy assets cheaply, but it had a similar effect on TMT stocks.

The Greek bond market was inconsequential in terms of size relative to global bonds, but it highlighted the interdependence that existed within the European financial system and helped produce the eurozone crisis. In each of these cases the cracks that appeared in the existing investor framework served to cause a reappraisal which led to violent downward shifts in asset prices.

In terms of the current environment, although the global scale and dominance of the US economy and US asset markets will make the US the epicentre of any future correction, it does not imply that the cracks will necessarily appear there first. Similarly, whilst sustained inflation would certainly pass pricing control of fixed-income products from the central banks back to the markets, it does not mean that inflation is the only mechanism or signal that could do so.

Whatever the prompt, the result at some point soon is likely to be disruption in asset markets. Investors currently take comfort from the fact that the world is awash with liquidity. My view is that this is a debt-created mirage. The liability side of the balance sheet – where all this liquidity comes from – is just as important and is being overlooked.

At some point liquidity will dry up. At some point too, government debt will be priced by markets rather than by the government. Valuations which have been supported by the suppressed 'risk-free' return on government securities will then have a rude awakening. It is a question of when, not whether, this happens.

There tends to be too much concentration on the question of what might trigger the event or be the catalyst for it unfolding. The answer is that it could be inflation, it could be default, it could be fears over market integrity and property rights. Equally it could be concern over debt funding and fiscal retrenchment.

It could easily be a mixture of all of the above or indeed some unforeseen exogenous event. But this is largely irrelevant. The reason asset prices will fall is that they are too high. In this environment, liquidity will evaporate, leaving few buyers in a market characterised by concern and uncertainty.

In the short run the response to falling asset prices and the perceived consequent threat to the economy will likely be additional government intervention/regulation. This will further undermine the market-pricing mechanism. These actions may well temporarily stick a finger in the dyke and hold asset prices for a while. Indeed, this may well be what is currently unfolding at the moment.

Eventually, however, the realisation that this is not a sustainable proposition will then lead investors to reappraise their investment framework accordingly – and this will produce a potentially devastating impact on prices. At that point the debt problem, wished away for years, will move back to centre stage.

In any scenario we will be living in a completely different world to that which we have experienced since the dawn of the Volcker-inspired bond and equity bull markets, reinforced as they have been by the positive secular trends in population, trade and market freedom.

Understanding how to invest in this environment means defining and understanding the new framework that will emerge and also understanding how different it will be from the one to which we have grown accustomed.

Be prepared!

What a new investing framework demands is an understanding of how the political and economic environment will unfold. At previous times of asset market stress there has typically been a tipping point at which the level of excess valuation has finally elevated to a point where gravity has caused a return to earth. This 'emperor's new clothes'-type moment has frequently been triggered by some fairly inconsequential event.

However, although the ripple effects of a bubble deflating spread wider than just the centre, the fact that there have always historically been assets whose valuations were nowhere near as stretched has tended to cushion the fall, allowing investors to take advantage of new opportunities that were also emerging. To take just one example, the seemingly endless decline of the Japanese stock market during the 1990s and beyond did not prevent other equity markets providing strong returns.

Within the Japanese market it was primarily the interest-rate-sensitive sectors, such as financials and real estate, which pulled down the indices. Within the falling indices you could still find undervalued companies.

However, the cost of money has never been sustained at artificially low levels for such a prolonged period before, nor across such a wide swathe of global markets. Nor have we seen an accumulation of debt on such a scale. Such has been the elevation of assets that some of the historical relationships between asset classes have been weakened or reversed. This has led to some particularly testing questions in portfolio design in terms of risk quantification.

It is no surprise that virtually every kind of investment asset has inflated to a greater or lesser degree in these unprecedented conditions. I am often asked what Sir John Templeton might have made of current conditions. This is very difficult to answer and somewhat presumptuous to try. It is first worth noting that Sir John was always nervous of economies where growth was fuelled by debt. In terms of responses on unusually high valuations the advice tended to be succinct. I can well remember approaching Sir John in 1997 after a research trip to Asia where my overwhelming impression was of excess optimism and unrealistic expectations. The consequence was that I simply could not find any cheap equities in the emerging markets. Sir John's response? "In my investing experience I have never found it sensible to buy expensive assets for clients."

In other words, the only thing that really mattered was whether asset prices were expensive or not. In the absence of attractive alternatives, his default position in professionally managed portfolios was to go to bonds or cash or other forms of liquidity. Capital preservation became the order of the day until prices corrected sufficiently to create meaningful new opportunities,[44] as they will always do in

---

44 Davis, J. and Nairn, A., 2012. *Templeton's Way with Money*. Wiley.

time. Unfortunately, government bonds – the traditional safe haven – have become virtually uninvestable at today's yields.

Sadly, Sir John is not around to offer any advice on how to navigate today's extreme currents, when there appear to be only small pockets of potential value with which to create positive real returns. Maybe this time it really is different! But if so, it is only different in the sense that we cannot find undervaluation. It is not different in the sense that buying expensive assets remains a poor long-term investment choice for clients.

While most fund managers are obliged to remain fully invested in their chosen strategy, come hell or high water, those who have the freedom to manage money more flexibly have a fiduciary duty to manage money in the best interests of their clients. They – we – are being faced with some tough choices.

The choices are tough because the options are so limited. Global listed equities are expensive. Private equity transactions are being executed at ever higher valuations with increasing debt and poorer covenants. Conventional government bonds have little attraction, given current yields. Inflation-linked bonds and gold have their supporters, but their fate also depends upon which of the several routes the authorities decide to take from here. Cash in currencies of less indebted nations with reasonable trade balances should retain value, but this will be eroded by inflation over the long-run and thus is a place of temporary respite to be reinvested when opportunities present themselves.

The truth is that until we know how the authorities will react to the inevitable future decline in equity markets, and can form a better judgment about the likely path of inflation and growth in the new conditions, patience is needed. Who knows, for example, if governments will resort in time to capital and interest-rate controls, as they did after the end of World War II? Or will they simply let inflation rip?

While being cognisant that precise timing of any downturn is well-nigh impossible, the first and most urgent requirement is to create a liquidity reserve which can quickly be deployed when there is sufficient clarity to understand what the new world will look like – and what the new investment framework will be after the end of the everything bubble.

Acknowledgements

THIS BOOK FOLLOWED a similar path to a number of previous writing exercises. Confronted by a set of conclusions which seemed obvious, it felt necessary to spend time considering whether there was some critical element that might be missing and could meaningfully change the logical outcome. The process of writing down the arguments and setting out the supporting data is a time-consuming and frustrating one, but it does have the useful tendency to highlight deficiencies and hence conclusions that may have been more emotion-driven, or arrived at without appropriate due diligence. This is not a journey that is easily followed on one's own. To successfully navigate it requires significant assistance. In this respect I am incredibly grateful to Jonathan Davis for his insights and patience, not to mention his ability to correct, edit and improve the various iterations of the text he was sent. Alan Bartlett possesses forensic analytical skills which were a huge assistance in keeping me on the straight and narrow and I know the analysis benefitted from the regular interactions I had with him. I am also grateful to Myles Hunt and Christopher Parker for putting up with me again and for helping take this through to a published form with their usual skill. I am also grateful to Franklin Templeton for fostering an environment which encourages the open debate of disparate views. Again, the contents of this book represent a personal view and should not be attributed to the Franklin Templeton organisation. Finally, I would be remiss to not mention the continued support I have had from my family and particularly from my wife who desperately tries not to roll her eyes when I say 'never again' as manuscripts are completed.